VEGAN HOLIDAY COOKING *from* CANDLE CAFE

——

VEGAN
HOLIDAY COOKING
from CANDLE CAFE

—

Celebratory Menus and Recipes from
New York's Premier Plant-Based Restaurants

JOY PIERSON, ANGEL RAMOS,
& JORGE PINEDA

Photography by Jim Franco

*Forewords by Alicia Silverstone and
Laura and Woody Harrelson*

TEN SPEED PRESS
Berkeley

In loving memory of Arlene Rosenberg DaSilva and Laksmi Magee,
who remind us that life is a party to be shared with those you love.

———————

Published in the United States by Ten Speed Press, an imprint
    of the Crown Publishing Group, a division of Random House LLC,
    a Penguin Random House Company, New York.
www.crownpublishing.com
www.tenspeed.com

Ten Speed Press and the Ten Speed Press colophon are registered trademarks
    of Random House LLC

Library of Congress Cataloging-in-Publication Data
Pierson, Joy.
    Vegan holiday cooking from Candle Cafe : celebratory menus and recipes from
    New York's premier plant-based restaurants / Joy Pierson, Angel Ramos, and Jorge Pineda.
        pages cm
    Summary: "Acclaimed vegan restaurants Candle Cafe and Candle 79
    present a collection of plant-based recipes for year-round holidays including
    Lunar New Year, Valentine's Day, Easter, Cinco de Mayo, Fourth of July,
    Thanksgiving, Passover, and Christmas"—
    Provided by publisher.
    1. Vegan cooking. 2. Holiday cooking. 3. Candle Cafe. 4. Candle 79 (Restaurant)
    I. Ramos, Angel, 1976- II. Pineda, Jorge. III. Title.
    TX837.P52936 2014
    641.5'636--dc23
                        2014005259

Hardcover ISBN: 978-1-60774-647-8
eBook ISBN: 978-1-60774-648-5

Printed in China

Food styling by Angel Ramos, Jorge Pineda, and Chris Barsch
Prop styling by Kate Parisian
Interior design by Hope Meng
Author photo by Eric Marseglia

10 9 8 7 6 5 4 3 2 1

First Edition

CONTENTS

Foreword

BY ALICIA SILVERSTONE

———

When I think of the Candles, I feel love. The entire Candle trio of restaurants, Candle Cafe, Candle 79, and Candle Cafe West, are the happiest, warmest, and most delicious places to be. They are all a reflection of the core—the Candle magic love potion—and I dare you not to get swept away by it.

All of the employees of each restaurant—from managers to busboys—are so welcoming and caring. And can we talk about Chefs Angel and Jorge? They are so talented, hardworking, warm, and super-cute, by the way. And whether they like it or not, I always go into the kitchen to give them big hugs and compliments after every spectacular meal that I've eaten there.

These transporting restaurants and their amazing food are the result of the vision of Joy and her husband and partner, Bart, both of whom I've known and loved for over thirteen years. Joy and I are crazy in love with food. We appreciate the fine, exquisite flavors of plant-based food and we love dishes that are made with passion, love, and care.

Joy and the Candle family know how to throw a great party. We have celebrated big and small dinners together and they have all been crazy yummy. For my thirtieth birthday party—hmm, a while back now—Joy and Bart sent Seitan Piccata to my home in California for forty guests. If you haven't tried it, you haven't lived. It is the best dish for a nonvegan eater to try. They catered backstage parties when I appeared on Broadway, sending trays of yummy plant-based goodies to the cast and crew and making us very happy. When I launched my line of eco-tool bags, they hosted business parties at their restaurants, serving food that had a mission that was in sync with mine and that deeply impressed a number of fashion editors. And a Candle Thanksgiving is a treat!

It's truly magical and special, full of fabulous tastes with no bad karma flying around the belly after dinner.

I am so thrilled that Joy, Angel, and Jorge decided to write a book devoted to cooking vegan for the holidays. In addition to the great menus and recipes, the photography and layout of this book are beautiful, and I want to make almost everything I see on these pages RIGHT NOW! Bravo!

This book is about celebration and fun—no deprivation, just pure joy and yumminess. It inspires me to plan a year of parties, and I am so eager to cook Joy's Grandma's seitan brisket and sweet potato latkes for Passover, and mini muffins and French toast coffeecake for my friends and all their kiddies for a spring brunch. There's the Cinco de Mayo fiesta (Bear's birthday) with crispy black bean tacos and caramel flan (I've had this at Candle 79 and it is insane!), and a cruelty-free backyard barbecue with grilled seitan burgers and spicy corn on the cob finished off with red, white, & blue shortcake. Maybe I'll have a holiday mash-up, serving the best of Thanksgiving and Christmas with a roasted brussels sprout salad, the polenta, mushroom, and kale casserole, Christmas spritz cookies, and a vegan cheese plate! OMG! And for Valentine's maybe I'll make a romantic dinner with roasted red pepper soup and dumplings, morel crusted tofu, and decadent molten chocolate cake. Seriously, I want to eat all of these things—right now.

I love Candle's commitment and passion for sustainability, for healing the planet with food and love. Thank God for the Candles and for Joy and Bart and Angel and Jorge.

And for this book. We are all so lucky to have this book. Let's get cookin'.

Love,
Alicia

Foreword

BY LAURA AND WOODY HARRELSON

———

We have worked and played and cooked and danced with Joy and Bart in our kitchens and theirs for over twenty years. We have dined on many fine, innovative meals, lasting many joyous hours, at all of the Candle establishments. These days, whenever we're in New York we always find a good excuse to throw a party and have it catered by the Candle Family. Our daughters have literally grown up with the Candle restaurants and a few summers ago our eldest was fortunate and smart enough to train with Chef Jorge, where she honed her kitchen and cooking skills.

We have such good karma with the Candle restaurants. We all first met at Bart's small shop The Healthy Candle and became close friends sharing the same mission and commitment. We have been in New York City for the openings of all three restaurants . . . Candle Cafe, Candle 79, and Candle Cafe West. Joy gives us credit for their success, which we happily accept. (As an actor, it's easy to accept credit for others' work!) But the real testament to their success is that their restaurants are always full of people, meat-eaters and vegetarians alike, enjoying the incredible vibes and delicious food.

In their over-the-top spirit of generosity, it comes as no great surprise that Joy, Bart, Angel, and Jorge offer this fine book for our entertaining-at-home pleasure. Traditionally, holidays are times spent overindulging and celebrating life. As it should be! There's no greater gift than to prepare beautiful meals that support and nurture health on every level for the folks we truly love. More research is released daily about the need for Americans and the world to shift to a healthier, plant-based diet. A growing number of Western doctors are recognizing the need to recommend plant-based diets to their patients as a form of treatment. When it evolves into lifestyle, the human body has a fighting chance to beat any disease. Good health is our birthright and we can take charge of it for our families and loved ones by recommitting ourselves over and over again to eating organic and vegan. And in this day and age, it doesn't mean we have to sacrifice taste. Fresh, organic food from farm to table has always been the Candle mantra and farm-fresh food always satisfies.

So pour your favorite drink or try one of the many fun ones inside *Vegan Holiday Cooking*, then do yourself a favor and sit down, put your feet up, and relax. Savor page after page of deliciously designed recipes that will tantalize your taste buds and feed and nourish the soul. From sexy cocktails (check out the Persephone and Chai Kiss Valentine's specialties) to decadent desserts (we can't wait to try the Strawberry Rhubarb Tarts with Vanilla Bean–Coconut Ice Cream!), you will want to cook this amazing food for every holiday. Better yet, why wait for a holiday to roll around? It's time to become host or hostess extraordinaire! No more excuses. Let the party begin!

With love and gratitude,
Laura and Woody

Introduction

We are always up for having a party. As we enter our thirtieth year of serving vegan cuisine at our three Candle restaurants in New York City, we have some pretty good ideas about how to throw one. In addition to running our restaurants, we have hosted and catered almost every kind of party imaginable—black-tie charity balls, celebrity weddings, rooftop cocktail parties, political fund-raisers, bar mitzvahs, children's birthday parties, and intimate home dinners, to name a few. No matter what the occasion, we always strive to bring along our own special brand of hospitality to these events with our creative, caring cuisine, organic wines, and sustainable specialty cocktails.

Over the years our friends, colleagues, loyal customers, and home cooks who share our passion for good food often ask for recipes from the restaurant to cook at home and for ideas for hosting parties and holiday dinners that feature vegan food. With *Vegan Holiday Cooking* we are thrilled to share our collective wealth of restaurant and catering expertise so you, too, can create delicious vegan food and creative cocktails for festive celebrations all year long.

Our talented and innovative cooks, led by executive chefs Angel Ramos and Jorge Pineda, are always expanding their cooking repertoires and have created many new, diverse, and delicious dishes that are sure to please vegans, vegetarians, and omnivores alike, especially for entertaining. They have created menus and recipes for a full year of festive holidays and occasions that will delight your friends and family—from a spicy Super Bowl party, to a "veganized" Passover seder, to a savory summer barbecue, to sumptuous Thanksgiving and Christmas dinners—all plant-based, extraordinary dishes that use every season's best and freshest ingredients. And since

holidays and celebrations always include family traditions, we've included recipes from our restaurant family, such as Joy's grandmother's brisket recipe for Passover (made with seitan, not meat), Candle founder Bart Potenza's Italian-influenced bruschetta, and Chef Angel's family secret for cooking perfect rice and beans. These dishes are hearty and filling, and we can attest that they will satisfy all of your guests, including the meat-eaters. This is rich and delicious holiday food, full of scrumptious flavor that is also healthful for body, mind, and soul.

In addition, our experienced crew of bartenders led by Gabriela Martinez Benecke has created a number of festive cocktails, elegant wine and champagne drinks, and party punches that are sure to inspire home mixologists. They're a lot fun to mix, share, and indulge in, and they pair beautifully with appetizers, finger foods, main courses, and desserts.

Most of the recipes in this book were developed to feed about ten guests, but they can be scaled back easily or doubled accordingly for smaller or larger groups. And since we know that it's important to plan ahead as much as possible for a party, many of our dishes, or parts of them, can be prepared well in advance of serving them.

Vegan Holiday Cooking is for people who love to cook and who are constantly looking for innovative and delicious recipes. It's for people who love to spend time in the kitchen, either alone or with friends, and create beautiful vegan food that is full of flavor and love. It's for cooks who love to bring everyone to the table to celebrate and savor the holidays. We are very happy and proud to share our food knowledge and ideas with you, and we know that you will enjoy cooking and sharing this food in your own home for your friends and family year-round. We invite you to come and celebrate with us!

THE VEGAN PANTRY

Most of the ingredients that you will need to cook our food are readily available at well-stocked supermarkets, international markets, and health food stores. We always use the freshest organic produce and fruits we can find at farmers' markets and good produce stores, and so should you. Our recipes use many other easy-to-find items like dried and canned beans; nuts; olive, safflower, sunflower, and grapeseed oils; assorted vinegars; and tofu. You may have to do some searching for seitan and tempeh, but they are usually available in health food stores. Nondairy products we often use include soy- and coconut-based milks and creamers, soy and tapioca cheeses, Earth Balance Natural Buttery Spread, and vegan cream cheese. For natural sweeteners, we like agave nectar, maple syrup, brown rice syrup, coconut sugar, and unrefined sugar. We also use the Ener-G brand of egg replacer in place of eggs. There is a resource guide for sourcing ingredients at the end of the book.

SUPER BOWL

BIG-GAME PARTY

———

Whether it's the Super Bowl, March Madness, the World Cup finals, or any other fierce competition, these events call for hearty eating and drinking while watching the big game. We like to serve a menu of scrumptious plant-based dishes like Roasted Poblano Guacamole and Wheat Ball Heroes along with a chili bar set up for our hungry guests to serve themselves and add their favorite garnishes. Drinks such as the Touchdown and the beer-based Frida round out this robust array of indulgent yet healthful food that scores a touchdown with the crowd every time.

THE FRIDA

Beer is essential at any Super Bowl party. Here is the Frida, a spicy, refreshing, beer-based drink that adds fresh lemon and orange juice, a few slices of jalapeño, and a healthy shot of tequila to the mix.

SERVES 1

½ ounce fresh lemon juice
1 ounce fresh orange juice
2 ounces tequila silver
2 thin jalapeño pepper slices, seeded
Ice
1 (12-ounce) bottle wheat beer
Pinch of sea salt
Pinch of cayenne pepper
1 twist orange peel, to garnish

Combine the lemon juice, orange juice, tequila, and jalapeño slices in a pilsner glass and stir with a bar spoon. Add ice and stir again. Pour in the beer to fill the glass, add salt and cayenne pepper, and stir again. Garnish with the orange peel and serve.

THE TOUCHDOWN

In this drink we use mezcal, a beverage that comes from the maguey plant, a form of agave. It has a unique smoky flavor that marries perfectly with bourbon. We recommend using the brand Ilegal Mezcal, because its smokiness is more vibrant than other mezcals we've tried.

SERVES 1

½ ounce mezcal
2 ounces bourbon
¾ ounce fresh lemon juice
¼ ounce fresh lime juice
½ ounce fresh orange juice
¼ ounce agave nectar
1 rosemary sprig, to garnish

Thoroughly rinse a rocks glass with the mezcal, let sit for 1 minute, and pour it out (or drink it, if you prefer.) In a large glass, combine the bourbon, lemon juice, lime juice, orange juice, and agave and stir. Fill the rocks glass with ice and pour the mixture into the glass. Garnish with the rosemary sprig and serve.

ROASTED POBLANO GUACAMOLE

Our version of guacamole is unique, and it always steals the show when we serve it. The secret to our fabulous guac is that we add slow-roasted poblano peppers to the creamy avocado blend. It adds a deep, rich, and unforgettable flavor. Serve with your favorite chips, breads, and crudités.

SERVES 8 TO 10

1 large poblano pepper
5 avocados, halved, pitted, peeled, and diced
2 tablespoons finely chopped red onion
2 tablespoons chopped plum tomato
2 teaspoons seeded and finely chopped jalapeño pepper
2 tablespoons finely chopped fresh cilantro
2 tablespoons fresh lime juice
1 teaspoon sea salt

Hold the poblano with a pair of metal tongs and roast over an open flame until it is brown all over, about 5 minutes. Put the poblano in a bowl, cover with plastic wrap, and let it steam for 5 minutes. Remove the plastic wrap, cover the pepper completely with water, and peel. Remove the poblano and discard the water. Split the pepper, remove all of the seeds, and finely chop.

In a clean bowl, combine the chopped poblano, avocados, red onion, tomato, jalapeño, cilantro, lime juice, and salt and mash together with a fork until smooth. Serve immediately.

CHOPPED VEGETABLE SALAD with GARDEN HERB RANCH DRESSING

We love the crunch of fresh lettuce, onions, cucumbers, and radishes in this gorgeous chopped salad that's topped with tofu feta and creamy, tangy ranch dressing. Because the healthful properties of the salad veggies balance all of the indulgent foods on the Game Night menu, this is just the right accompaniment. The tofu feta has to marinate overnight, so plan accordingly.

SERVES 8 TO 10

TOFU FETA

1 (14-ounce) block extra-firm tofu
¼ cup fresh lemon juice
1 teaspoon dried basil
1 teaspoon dried oregano
1 teaspoon garlic powder
½ teaspoon smoked paprika
1 tablespoon sea salt
Pinch of freshly ground black pepper

RANCH DRESSING

1 tablespoon brown mustard
1 tablespoon apple cider vinegar
½ cup vegan mayonnaise
¼ cup fresh lemon juice
1 teaspoon garlic powder
1 teaspoon onion powder
2 tablespoons extra-virgin olive oil
½ teaspoon chopped fresh flat-leaf parsley
½ teaspoon chopped fresh oregano

½ teaspoon chopped fresh thyme
Fine sea salt and freshly ground black pepper

2 small heads romaine lettuce, outer leaves removed
Fine sea salt and freshly ground black pepper
1 small red onion, thinly sliced
2 medium cucumbers, peeled and diced
2 cups cooked corn kernels
1½ cups grape tomatoes, halved
1½ cups drained and chopped canned hearts of palm
4 radishes, thinly sliced
¾ cup kalamata olives, pitted and sliced
3 tablespoons chopped fresh chives

To make the tofu feta, the day before serving, drain the tofu and cut into cubes. Fill a 3-quart saucepan with 1 quart of water and bring to a boil. Add the tofu, decrease the heat, and simmer over medium heat for about 8 minutes. Drain the tofu, transfer to a bowl, and set aside.

Whisk the lemon juice, basil, oregano, garlic powder, paprika, and salt and pepper together in a small bowl and pour over the tofu. Cover and let marinate in the refrigerator for at least 8 hours, or overnight.

To make the dressing, whisk together the mustard, vinegar, vegan mayonnaise, lemon juice, garlic powder, and onion powder in a bowl. Slowly drizzle in the olive oil, whisking constantly, until smooth and well blended. Stir in the parsley, oregano, thyme, and salt and pepper to taste. Cover and refrigerate for at least 1 hour.

To assemble the salad, chop the lettuce into bite-size pieces and transfer to a large bowl. Pour about two-thirds of the dressing over the lettuce and toss together, adding salt and pepper to taste.

Drain the tofu feta, crumble it, and sprinkle it over the salad. Add the onion, cucumbers, corn, tomatoes, hearts of palm, radishes, olives, and chives and toss with the remaining dressing. Taste and adjust the seasonings, if necessary, and serve immediately.

MAKE YOUR OWN CHILI BOWL

Hearty chili cooked with French lentils and smoky spices like paprika, chili powder, and chipotle chile powder is a robust, satisfying dish to feed to a hungry crowd. To accompany the chili, we put out a big spread of garnishes—Roasted Poblano Guacamole (page 7), chopped bell peppers, green onions, red onions, parsley, cilantro, salsa, and tofu sour cream, to name a few— and let our guests help themselves.

SERVES 8 TO 10

1 cup French lentils, rinsed and drained
2 teaspoons sea salt
2 tablespoons extra-virgin olive oil
2 cups chopped yellow onions
1 red bell pepper, seeded and diced
1 green bell pepper, seeded and diced
2 cloves garlic, chopped
½ teaspoon ground cumin
½ teaspoon smoked paprika
½ teaspoon chipotle chile powder
½ teaspoon chili powder
½ teaspoon fresh oregano
4 cups diced tomatoes or 2 (14-ounce) cans diced tomatoes
4 cups tomato juice
2 (15.5-ounce) cans red kidney beans, drained and rinsed

Guacamole, salsa, tofu sour cream, chopped bell peppers, green onions, red onions, parsley, and cilantro, to garnish

Place the lentils in a large saucepan. Add 8 cups of water and 1 teaspoon of the salt. Bring to a boil, decrease the heat, and cook over medium-high heat until tender, 15 to 20 minutes. Drain and set aside.

Heat the olive oil in a large soup pot over medium-high heat; add the onions, bell peppers, and garlic and cook for 7 to 10 minutes, until the onions are translucent. Add the cumin, paprika, chipotle powder, chili powder, oregano, and remaining teaspoon of salt and stir well. Cook for 1 to 2 minutes, stirring, until all of the spices are incorporated.

Add the tomatoes and tomato juice to the pot and simmer for 15 to 20 minutes, until the liquid reduces and the chili thickens up. Add the lentils and kidney beans and simmer for an additional 10 minutes. (At this point, you can store the chili in the refrigerator for up to 3 days ahead of time, or freeze for up to 1 month. Bring the chili to room temperature before reheating.)

Serve the chili warm with garnishes on the side.

WHEAT BALL HEROES

Wheat balls are a signature dish at all of our Candle restaurants, and we often stuff them into hero sandwiches topped with a chunky red sauce and vegan mozzarella cheese to make a lighter, vegan version of the Italian classic. Dig into these warm and crunchy sandwiches when they're just out of the oven. Mangia!

SERVES 8

CHUNKY MARINARA SAUCE
¼ cup extra-virgin olive oil
2 cups diced yellow onions
8 cloves garlic, minced
1 teaspoon fresh oregano
1 teaspoon red pepper flakes
2 (28-ounce) cans plum tomatoes or 12 large red tomatoes, chopped
Sea salt and freshly ground black pepper

SEITAN BALLS
2 tablespoons extra-virgin olive oil
1 cup chopped red onion
2 teaspoons minced garlic
2 teaspoons dried oregano
2 pounds seitan, drained and cut into 1-inch chunks
2 cups dried bread crumbs
½ cup chopped fresh flat-leaf parsley
1 teaspoon sea salt
1 teaspoon freshly ground black pepper

2 baguettes, split lengthwise
12 slices soy or tapioca mozzarella

To make the sauce, heat the olive oil in a pot over medium-high heat, add the onions, and sauté until translucent, about 10 minutes. Add the garlic, oregano, and pepper flakes and stir for a minute.

Add the tomatoes and bring to a boil, decrease the heat, and simmer over medium-low heat for 30 to 40 minutes, stirring occasionally, until the sauce reduces and thickens up. Add salt and pepper to taste. Remove from the heat and let cool.

Transfer half of the sauce to a blender and blend until smooth. Return to pot and stir together. The sauce will keep in the refrigerator, covered, for up to 1 week. It can be frozen for a month. Reheat the sauce before serving.

Preheat the oven to 350°F. Oil a baking sheet.

To make the wheat balls, heat the olive oil in a sauté pan over medium heat. Add the onion and garlic and sauté until softened, about 5 minutes. Add the oregano and cook, stirring, for 1 minute.

Combine the onion mixture, seitan, bread crumbs, parsley, salt, and pepper in a food processor and blend until incorporated. This may have to be done in batches.

Using 2 tablespoons of the seitan mixture, shape into balls and arrange on the prepared baking sheet just far enough apart that they are not touching. Bake for 30 to 40 minutes, until lightly browned, turning them after 20 minutes. Set aside.

Increase the oven temperature to 400°F. Arrange the baguettes on a baking sheet, pressing them open. Layer the bottom halves with the wheat balls, tomato sauce, and cheese. Put the heroes in the oven and bake until the cheese is melted and the sandwiches are warmed through, 3 to 5 minutes, making sure not to burn the bread. Press the top halves over the bottom halves, cut each baguette into quarters, and serve warm.

SEITAN and TEMPEH FINGERS with SWEET MUSTARD DIPPING SAUCE

We love to serve these crunchy fried fingers of seitan and tempeh with a tangy mustard dipping sauce. Even though these snacks are salty, satisfying, and delicious, you can eat them without feeling too guilty because they are loaded with nutritious protein and complex carbs. Note that when you prepare the tempeh, it needs to parboil in water and tamari before pan-frying.

SERVES 8 TO 10

SWEET MUSTARD DIPPING SAUCE
1 cup brown mustard
3 tablespoons agave nectar
½ teaspoon unrefined sugar
½ teaspoon hot sauce
Pinch of sea salt

2 (8-ounce) packages tempeh, cut into 2- to 3-inch-long strips
2 tablespoons tamari
1 tablespoon peeled and chopped fresh ginger
1 tablespoon grapeseed oil
3 bay leaves
6 cilantro sprigs
2 cups yellow cornmeal
½ cup dried bread crumbs
2 tablespoons Ener-G egg replacer
1 tablespoon smoked paprika
½ teaspoon sea salt
½ teaspoon freshly ground black pepper
2 cups plain unsweetened soy milk
1 pound seitan, cut into 2- to 3-inch-long strips
1 cup safflower oil

To make the dipping sauce, whisk together the mustard, agave, sugar, hot sauce, and salt in a bowl. Taste and adjust the seasonings, if necessary. The sauce will keep, covered, in the refrigerator for up to 3 days. Bring to room temperature before serving.

To prepare the tempeh, combine 8 cups of water in a pot with the tempeh, tamari, ginger, grapeseed oil, bay leaves, and cilantro; simmer over medium-low heat for 15 minutes. Drain, discard the bay leaf and cilantro, and set aside.

Combine the cornmeal, bread crumbs, egg replacer, paprika, salt, and pepper in a large bowl. Mix together and set aside. Pour the soy milk into another bowl.

Dip the tempeh strips in the soy milk to cover each piece completely. Shake off the excess liquid. Dredge the strips in the cornmeal mixture and transfer to a plate. Repeat this process with the seitan strips.

Heat ½ cup of the oil in a large sauté pan over medium heat. Add the tempeh strips and fry them until golden brown, 3 to 5 minutes per side. Drain on paper towels. Add the remaining ½ cup oil, heat, and fry the seitan strips until golden brown, about 2 minutes. Drain on paper towels. Serve immediately with the dipping sauce on the side.

STOUT BROWNIES

Beer and chocolate are a winning combo, and these tasty brownies made with stout are a delicious way to wrap up the party. Add homemade French Vanilla Ice Cream (page 17) to really wow the game day crowd. These brownies are fun to serve for St. Patrick's Day, too!

Look for good vegan stouts and porter beers like Samuel Smith Brewery's Imperial Stout, Oatmeal Stout, and Chocolate Stout, or Butte Creek Porter. When shopping for vegan chocolate chips, we recommend buying small ones—Enjoy Life and Sunspire are good brands—because they melt quickly and evenly.

MAKES 18 TO 20 BROWNIES

¾ cup brown rice syrup
1½ cups small vegan semisweet chocolate chips
½ cup plain unsweetened soy milk
¾ cup Earth Balance Natural Buttery Spread
½ cup maple syrup
2½ cups unbleached all-purpose flour
½ cup natural cocoa powder
1 tablespoon baking powder
¼ cup Ener-G egg replacer
¼ cup pureed silken tofu
½ teaspoon sea salt
½ cup stout or porter beer

Preheat the oven to 350°F. Oil a 9 by 13-inch baking dish.

Combine the brown rice syrup, chocolate chips, soy milk, buttery spread, and maple syrup in a double boiler over simmering water and stir until melted. Set aside and let cool.

Stir the flour, cocoa powder, baking powder, egg replacer, pureed tofu, and salt in a large bowl until smooth. Pour in the chocolate mixture. Slowly pour in the stout and stir until smooth. Spread the mixture evenly into the prepared baking dish.

Bake for about 30 minutes, until the top is no longer shiny and a cake tester comes out clean. Let the brownies cool for at least 20 minutes before cutting them into squares. They are best served fresh but will keep, covered, for a day or two.

ICE CREAM SANDWICHES

These ice cream sandwiches are lots of fun for both kids and grown-ups to make and eat. The cookies are just the right size for little hands. Be sure to coat these treats with chocolate chips, sprinkles, or chopped nuts to make them even yummier.

MAKES 8 ICE CREAM SANDWICHES

FRENCH VANILLA ICE CREAM

1 cup plain unsweetened soy milk
1 cup soy creamer
¼ cup safflower oil
1½ teaspoons vanilla extract
½ cup unrefined sugar
2 cups coconut milk

COOKIES

¾ cup Earth Balance Natural Buttery Spread
1½ cups unrefined sugar
5 ounces silken tofu
1½ teaspoons vanilla extract
¾ teaspoon baking soda dissolved in 1 teaspoon hot water
¾ teaspoon sea salt
2¼ cups unbleached all-purpose flour
2 cups vegan chocolate chips, sprinkles, or crushed nuts, to garnish

To make the ice cream, combine the soy milk, soy creamer, safflower oil, vanilla extract, sugar, and coconut milk in a blender and blend for 1 minute.

Transfer the mixture to an ice cream maker and freeze according to manufacturer's directions. Remove and store in a bowl in the freezer for at least an hour and up to a week.

Preheat the oven to 350°F. Oil a baking sheet.

To make the cookies, cream together the buttery spread and sugar in a large bowl until smooth. Add the tofu, vanilla, baking soda mixture, and salt and stir together. Add the flour and stir together. Chill the cookie dough for 30 minutes.

Arrange 1½-inch balls of the dough on the prepared baking sheet about 3 inches apart and flatten them with a spatula to make 4-inch-diameter circles. Bake for about 18 minutes, until golden brown. Remove from the oven and let cool on the baking sheet.

To assemble the cookie sandwiches, put a scoop of ice cream on the flat bottom of a cookie. Press down with a spatula to flatten. Put another cookie on top, flat side down, and press down to make it stick and further flatten the ice cream.

Roll the exposed ice cream edges in the desired toppings to coat. Serve immediately.

LUNAR NEW YEAR

Lunar New Year is observed throughout all of Asia and in Asian neighborhoods in the States. Its date is determined by the cycles of the moon, and it usually falls in late January or early February. The holiday celebrates a hope for happiness, health, prosperity, and longevity. We celebrate by serving traditional dim sum dishes like dumplings and scallion pancakes, along with soba noodles, ginger braised tofu, and sweet and simple desserts. This light and tasty fare most certainly will bring you health and happiness.

DUILIAN

Duilians are bright red and gold scrolls that are used as decorations during the Lunar New Year, and they express hopeful and uplifting messages. Although you can use any brand of spiced rum, we prefer organic Crusoe. Enjoy this flavorful and spicy cocktail and drink to a happy and healthy new year.

SERVES 1

1½ ounces spiced rum
1 ounce coconut milk
1½ ounces pineapple juice
½ ounce agave nectar
¼ ounce ginger juice
4 basil leaves

Combine the rum, coconut milk, pineapple juice, agave, and ginger juice in a cocktail shaker. Tear 3 of the basil leaves into small pieces and add to the shaker. Shake well and pour into a rocks glass. Garnish with the remaining basil leaf and serve.

DAIDAI

This cocktail has bitter and sweet notes like its namesake, the daidai, a bitter Japanese orange that is used as a decoration for the Japanese New Year. This libation's warming effect is great on a cold winter's day.

SERVES 1

1½ ounces vodka
1½ ounces dry sake
½ ounce orange liqueur
¼ ounce maple syrup
¼ ounce ginger juice
Ice
Lemon peel, to garnish

Combine the vodka, sake, orange liqueur, maple syrup, and ginger juice in a cocktail shaker. Add ice, shake well, and strain into a martini glass.

To flame the lemon peel, hold a lit match close to the outer side of the lemon peel for about 2 seconds and squeeze the lemon peel on top of the flame facing the glass. The oils should be released from the outer side of the peel into the cocktail, creating a small flame.

Garnish with the flamed lemon peel and serve.

GRILLED BOK CHOY with SESAME-GINGER SAUCE

Bok choy is a very healthful vegetable, and we serve it at our restaurants in a number of ways—steamed, sautéed, and stir-fried. Here we grill it and toss with a sauce that's packed with the flavors of miso, ginger, green onions, and sesame oil. This dish comes together quickly and complements a variety of Asian dishes.

SERVES 8 TO 10

SESAME-GINGER SAUCE
½ cup water
3 tablespoons white miso
1½ teaspoons tamari
2 tablespoons brown rice vinegar
½ teaspoon toasted sesame oil
2 tablespoons peeled and finely diced ginger
⅓ cup chopped green onions, white and green parts
½ teaspoon white sesame seeds
¼ teaspoon red pepper flakes
¼ teaspoon chopped garlic

1 tablespoon extra-virgin olive oil
2 pounds baby bok choy heads, halved lengthwise

To make the sauce, combine the water, miso, tamari, vinegar, and sesame oil in a blender and blend for 3 minutes. Transfer to a bowl and add the ginger, green onions, sesame seeds, red pepper flakes, and garlic. Stir together and set aside.

Heat a large grill pan over medium-high heat and brush with the olive oil. Add the bok choy and grill both sides until tender, 2 to 3 minutes per side.

Transfer the bok choy to a bowl, add the sesame-ginger sauce, toss together, and serve.

STEAMED VEGETABLE DUMPLINGS with GINGER-SOY DIPPING SAUCE

Steamed dumplings are terrific appetizers for all ages, and they are a perfect party food to pass around on trays. We love the combination of tastes and textures in the vegetable filling, dumpling skins, and dipping sauce. Look for vegan dumpling wrappers in health food stores and Asian specialty shops. Note: To freeze uncooked dumplings, arrange them on a baking sheet and put in the freezer. Once they're frozen, put them in a plastic bag. They can be cooked frozen, but the cooking time will be a bit longer.

SERVES 8 TO 10; MAKES ABOUT 42 DUMPLINGS

GINGER-SOY DIPPING SAUCE
¼ cup soy sauce
1 tablespoon rice wine vinegar
1 teaspoon peeled and shredded fresh ginger
1 teaspoon toasted sesame oil
¼ teaspoon red pepper flakes

2 cups chopped broccoli florets
2 cups shredded green cabbage
1 cup shredded carrots
1 cup fresh or frozen and thawed green peas
3 green onions, white and green parts, chopped
2 tablespoons white miso paste
1 tablespoon tamari sauce
2 cloves garlic, coarsely chopped
1 teaspoon peeled and minced fresh ginger
½ teaspoon toasted sesame oil
42 vegan wonton wrappers

¼ cup toasted sesame seeds, to garnish
½ cup chopped green onions, white and green parts,
  to garnish

To make the dipping sauce, whisk together the soy sauce, rice wine vinegar, ginger, sesame oil, and red pepper flakes in a small bowl. Set aside.

Combine the broccoli, cabbage, carrots, peas, green onions, miso paste, tamari, garlic, and ginger in a food processor and blend until coarsely chopped.

Heat the sesame oil in a large skillet over medium heat. Add the vegetable mixture and cook, stirring, until softened, about 5 minutes. Set aside and let cool.

Keep the package of wonton wrappers covered with a damp cloth so the wrappers don't dry out. To assemble the dumplings, spoon about 1 tablespoon of the filling on half of the wrapper. Using a brush or your fingers, dampen the edges of the unfilled side of the wrapper with water. Fold in half on the diagonal and firmly pinch the edges to form a triangle, making sure that the dumpling is completely sealed. Repeat with the remaining wrappers and filling. Arrange them on a baking sheet lined with parchment paper until you are ready to boil them.

Fill a large pot halfway with water and bring to a boil. Using a slotted spoon, drop in a few dumplings and boil until the dumplings float to the top, about 5 minutes, stirring occasionally to keep them separate. Remove and drain. Repeat with the remaining dumplings until all are cooked.

Garnish the dumplings with sesame seeds and green onions and serve with the dipping sauce.

SOBA NOODLE and SEAWEED SALAD with WASABI-TAHINI DRESSING

Soba noodles are usually made with a combination of buckwheat and wheat, but there are also gluten-free options available such as yam, ginger, and pure buckwheat noodles. We always make a generous amount of the wasabi dressing and use any extra for livening up vegetables, rice, and salads.

SERVES 8 TO 10

WASABI-TAHINI DRESSING
1 cup water
2 tablespoons wasabi paste or powder
⅓ cup tahini
3 tablespoons brown rice vinegar
1 tablespoon umeboshi vinegar
½ teaspoon toasted sesame oil
2 tablespoons chopped green onions, white and green parts
1 tablespoon peeled and finely chopped fresh ginger

1 (4-ounce) package dried mixed seaweed
1 (8-ounce) package soba noodles
1 red bell pepper, seeded and cut into thin strips
½ cup chopped green onions, white and green parts
1 tablespoon white sesame seeds
1 tablespoon black sesame seeds

To make the dressing, combine the water, wasabi paste, tahini, rice vinegar, umeboshi vinegar, sesame oil, and green onions in a blender and blend until smooth, 3 to 5 minutes. Transfer to a bowl and stir in the ginger. Cover and refrigerate for at least 30 minutes.

Meanwhile, put the seaweed in a large bowl, add 4 cups of cold water, and let soak for 1 hour. Rinse thoroughly, drain, and set aside.

Bring 4 cups of water to a boil in a large pot. Add the soba noodles and cook for 7 minutes. Drain and rinse with cold water.

Transfer the noodles to a large bowl and add the seaweed, red pepper, green onions, and sesame seeds and toss together. Pour half of the dressing over the noodles and toss together.

Serve the noodles in a large bowl and drizzle more dressing over them, if desired.

MISO-GINGER BRAISED TOFU over BAMBOO RICE PILAF

This is an exquisite dish where miso and fresh ginger infuse tofu in a subtle and delicious way. The tofu is served with stir-fried vegetables in a savory bamboo rice pilaf. If you can't find bamboo rice, use white or brown jasmine rice.

SERVES 8

2 (14-ounce) blocks extra-firm tofu
3 tablespoons white miso
2 tablespoons peeled and finely chopped fresh ginger
1½ teaspoons ginger juice
1 bunch green onions, white and green parts, chopped
1 tablespoon chopped fresh basil
1 tablespoon chopped fresh mint
1 tablespoon agave nectar or unrefined sugar
2 tablespoons tamari
2 tablespoons brown rice vinegar
1 tablespoon umeboshi vinegar
2 tablespoons grapeseed oil
2 cups water

RICE PILAF

2½ cups water
2 cups bamboo rice
2 tablespoons grapeseed oil, plus more if needed
½ cup diced carrot
½ cup diced yellow onion
½ cup seeded and diced red bell pepper
1 tablespoon tamari
1 tablespoon brown rice vinegar

Preheat the oven to 350°F.

To prepare the tofu, drain and slice each tofu block into 4 equal pieces and pat with paper towels to remove any excess water.

Combine the miso, ginger, ginger juice, green onions, basil, mint, agave, tamari, brown rice vinegar, umeboshi vinegar, grapeseed oil, and water in a blender and blend until smooth, 3 to 5 minutes.

Put the sliced tofu in a 9 by 13-inch baking dish. Pour the miso-ginger mixture over the tofu and turn the pieces to coat. Cover the pan with aluminum foil and bake for 30 minutes. Uncover and cook for an additional 10 minutes until lightly browned on top.

To make the pilaf, bring the water to a boil over medium-high heat in a large saucepan and add the rice. Decrease the heat to medium-low, cover, and cook until all of the water is absorbed, 20 to 25 minutes. Remove from the heat and let sit.

Heat the oil in a sauté pan over medium-high heat. Add the carrot, onion, and bell pepper and sauté until tender, about 5 minutes.

Add the vegetables to the rice. Add the tamari and brown rice vinegar and stir together. If the rice seems sticky, add a bit more oil.

To serve, spoon the rice onto plates or a platter, top with the tofu, and drizzle with the pan juices.

MAPLE-ROASTED KABOCHA SQUASH and PICKLED LOTUS ROOT

*Like many winter squashes, kabocha calls for cutting up
with a very sharp knife and some elbow grease, but its
naturally sweet flavor makes it all worth it. Here we top
it with crunchy pickled lotus root that adds a wonderfully piquant flavor note to the dish.*

SERVES 8 TO 10

PICKLED LOTUS ROOT

4 cups water
¼ cup brown rice vinegar
2 tablespoons apple cider vinegar
2 tablespoons unrefined sugar
1 tablespoon sea salt
½ teaspoon ground turmeric
8 ounces lotus root, peeled and thinly sliced

1 large or 2 small kabocha squash
3 tablespoons maple syrup
1 tablespoon peeled and chopped fresh ginger
½ teaspoon freshly ground black pepper
2 tablespoons extra-virgin olive oil

To make the pickled lotus root, combine the water, brown
rice vinegar, cider vinegar, sugar, salt, and turmeric in a
saucepan and bring to a boil. Add the lotus root and cook
over medium-high heat for 5 minutes. Remove the pan
from the heat and let the mixture sit for 1 hour.

Remove the lotus root from the liquid and set aside. (If
you are not using it right away, store the lotus root in its
liquid, covered, in the refrigerator for up to 2 days.)

Preheat the oven to 350°F. Oil a large baking sheet.

To prepare the squash, with a sharp knife, trim the top
and bottom from the squash and cut it in half. Scoop out
the seeds and cut the flesh into thin wedges. Peel off the
skin with a sharp vegetable peeler, if desired.

Combine the squash, maple syrup, ginger, pepper, and
olive oil in a large bowl and toss together. Transfer to
the baking sheet and cover with aluminum foil.

Roast the squash for 15 minutes, remove the foil,
and return the squash to the oven to roast for 10 to
15 minutes more, until tender.

To serve, arrange the squash on a platter and spoon
the lotus root over the top.

SWEET FRIED DUMPLINGS with BLOOD ORANGE–GINGER SAUCE

Your guests will love these tempting little treats. Beautiful crimson blood oranges and ginger blend together to make a wonderfully tart sauce for the crispy sweet dumplings filled with melted chocolate. We make the sauce often in the winter months, when blood oranges are available, and drizzle it over ice cream, sorbet, and poached fruit.

SERVES 8 TO 10; MAKES 36 TO 40 DUMPLINGS

CHOCOLATE FILLING
3 cups vegan semisweet chocolate chips
½ cup plain unsweetened soy milk
2 tablespoons silken tofu
1 teaspoon maple syrup

BLOOD ORANGE–GINGER SAUCE
1 cup fresh blood orange juice
½ cup agave nectar
2 tablespoons peeled and chopped fresh ginger
½ teaspoon arrowroot powder

40 vegan wonton wrappers
Safflower oil, for frying
Confectioners' sugar, to serve

To make the filling, combine the chocolate chips and soy milk in a medium saucepan and cook over medium-low heat until melted. Let cool and transfer to a blender. Add the tofu and maple syrup and blend until smooth. Pour into a bowl and let cool in the refrigerator for 2 hours.

To make the sauce, combine the orange juice, agave, and ginger in a small saucepan over medium heat and cook, stirring, for 3 minutes. Add the arrowroot and cook for 1 minute. Remove from the heat and let cool.

To assemble the dumplings, lay a wrapper on a clean surface. Put a tablespoon of the filling in the center. With your finger, wipe the wrapper with water all around the filling. Bring two opposite corners up around the filling and pinch together tightly to make a triangle. Fold the lower corners of the wrapper in, twisting the lower corners together, making sure that all sides of the wrapper are sealed. Gently push the dumpling down to form a flat bottom.

Heat 1 inch of the oil in a large sauté pan over medium-high heat and, working in batches, fry the dumplings, turning often, until golden brown, 3 to 4 minutes. Remove them with a slotted spoon and drain on paper towels. Repeat with the remaining dumplings, adding more oil as necessary.

To serve, arrange the dumplings on a plate, dust with confectioners' sugar, and serve with the blood orange sauce on the side for dipping.

SAKE-LIME SORBET with TOASTED COCONUT

Sake is usually thought of as a drink to accompany Asian food, but it is a surprisingly good ingredient to add to coconut, fresh lime juice, and agave to make refreshing sorbet. Topped with toasted coconut, it tastes as beautiful as it looks, and we love to serve this light and tangy dessert all year-round.

MAKES 1 QUART

1 cup coconut water
½ cup fresh lime juice
¼ cup sake
1 cup baby Thai coconut meat or ½ cup creamed coconut
1 cup agave nectar
¼ cup dried unsweetened shredded coconut

Preheat the oven to 300°F.

Combine the coconut water, lime juice, sake, coconut meat, and agave in a blender and blend until smooth.

Transfer the mixture to an ice cream maker and freeze according to the manufacturer's directions. Remove and store in a bowl in the freezer for at least an hour and up to a week.

Put the shredded coconut on a baking sheet and bake for about 7 minutes, until golden brown.

To serve, scoop the sorbet into bowls and sprinkle each serving with the toasted coconut.

HERBAL TEA of GOOD FORTUNE

This brew is made with both lemon verbena tea and lemon myrtle leaves. Lemon myrtle leaves come from an Australian tree, and they have a pronounced spicy lemon flavor. Look for them in health food stores. Drinking this tea is a wonderful part of our Lunar New Year celebration, and it is sure to start your year off right. Happy New Year and many tea blessings.

SERVES 8 TO 10

4 tablespoons lemon verbena tea leaves
4 tablespoons green tea leaves
3 tablespoons peeled and finely chopped fresh ginger
4 ounces rose hips, seeded and cut
6 tablespoons chopped lemongrass
2 teaspoons chopped dried lemon myrtle
4 quarts water

Combine the lemon verbena and green tea leaves, ginger, rose hips, lemongrass, and lemon myrtle in a bowl and mix together.

Bring the water to a boil in a large teapot or a pan and then turn off heat. Once the bubbling has stopped, add the tea mixture and steep for 3 minutes. Strain the tea through a fine-mesh strainer into mugs or pour into a teapot and strain from there into teacups.

VALENTINE'S DAY

We love love and celebrate it every day, but on Valentine's
Day we pull out all the stops and create a sumptuous,
enticing menu to warm and nourish the heart. From our Chai
Kiss cocktail to our Passion Fruit Crème Brûlée, this meal is
truly a love potion. And if you're making it for just you and
your sweetheart, you'll likely have enough left over to relax
and enjoy the fruits of your labor the next day as well.

PERSEPHONE

One of the special cocktails we serve to the happy couples in our restaurant on Valentine's Day is named for Persephone, the harvest goddess. Although it can be made with any type of gin, we use Greenhook Gin, a dry American gin that is made in Greenpoint, Brooklyn. It has a unique, lively flavor with hints of elderflower, chamomile, and ginger.

SERVES 1

2 ounces gin
1 ounce elderflower liqueur
½ ounce rose water
½ ounce VeeV açai spirit
Ice
Dash of cherry bitters
Pomegranate seeds, to garnish

Combine the gin, elderflower liqueur, rose water, and açai liqueur in a large mixing glass. Add ice, stir well, and strain into a martini glass. Add the bitters, garnish with pomegranate seeds, and serve.

CHAI KISS

This is another special concoction that is lovely to serve for Valentine's Day. We use Fair vodka, a quinoa-based vodka that has a delicate, smooth flavor with notes of spice. If you're feeling extravagant and romantic, garnish your sweetheart's drink with an edible orchid (which you can find online).

SERVES 1

Ice
2 ounces vodka
1 teaspoon brewed chai tea
Splash of maple syrup
1 ounce pomegranate juice
1 ounce fresh lemon juice
1 ounce agave nectar
Splash of dry vermouth
Lemon peel twist, to garnish
Edible orchid, to garnish (optional)

Fill a cocktail shaker with ice, and add the vodka, tea, maple syrup, pomegranate juice, lemon juice, and agave and shake well.

Rinse a martini glass with dry vermouth. Strain the drink into the prepared glass.

Garnish with the lemon twist and orchid and serve.

ROASTED RED PEPPER SOUP with TOFU DUMPLINGS

The delicious prelude to this romantic dinner is a rich and smooth soup made with roasted red peppers and topped with succulent, plump tofu dumplings. The dumplings cook quickly in the simmering soup, so be sure not to overcook them.

SERVES 4 TO 6

4 red bell peppers
3 tablespoons extra-virgin olive oil
½ cup finely chopped yellow onion
½ cup finely chopped leeks, white and green parts
½ cup fresh or frozen corn kernels, thawed if frozen
3 cups vegetable stock or water
½ teaspoon sea salt, plus more if needed
¼ teaspoon freshly ground black pepper,
  plus more if needed
10 basil leaves, finely chopped
½ cup fresh or frozen English peas, thawed if frozen

TOFU DUMPLINGS
1 (14-ounce) block extra-firm tofu
1 tablespoon fresh lemon juice
1 tablespoon nutritional yeast
1 tablespoon extra-virgin olive oil
1 teaspoon sea salt
1 bunch green onions, white and green parts, chopped
24 vegan wonton wrappers

Preheat the oven to 350°F.

To make the soup, coat the peppers in 1 tablespoon of the olive oil, put them on a baking sheet, and roast for 30 to 40 minutes, until softened. When cool enough to handle, peel and seed the peppers, transfer to a blender, and blend until smooth.

Heat the remaining 2 tablespoons of the olive oil in a soup pot over medium heat, add the onion and leeks, and cook for 5 minutes. Add the corn and cook for 5 minutes. Add the pepper puree and stock and simmer for 15 minutes. Add salt and pepper and simmer for 5 more minutes.

Meanwhile, to prepare the dumplings, cut the tofu into small pieces and set in a steamer over simmering water. Steam the tofu for 10 minutes. Drain and let cool.

Combine the tofu, lemon juice, nutritional yeast, olive oil, and salt in a food processor and blend until smooth. Transfer the mixture to a bowl and add the green onions.

Spoon a teaspoon of the tofu filling into the center of each wonton wrapper. Brush the edge of each wonton wrapper with water. Fold over and press the edges together firmly to form a triangle.

Bring the soup to a low simmer, add half of the basil, the dumplings, and peas and cook until the dumplings are just tender, 2 to 3 minutes. Add more salt and pepper to taste, if desired.

To serve, ladle the soup and dumplings into soup bowls and garnish each serving with some of the remaining basil. Leftover soup will keep in the refrigerator for up to 4 days.

MÂCHE and ENDIVE SALAD with CREAMY AVOCADO VINAIGRETTE

Made with mâche, endive, hearts of palm, and artichokes, drizzled with creamy avocado vinaigrette, and garnished with blood oranges, this salad is an elegant special-occasion appetizer. Blood oranges are in season December through April and are the perfect shade for a Valentine's Day salad, but if they're not available, use navel oranges. Note that you'll want to refrigerate extra salad and dressing separately for tossing together just before eating the next day.

SERVES 4 TO 6

2 medium artichokes
1 (14-ounce) can hearts of palm, drained and chopped
8 ounces mâche
2 heads endive, torn into bite-sized pieces
2 blood oranges, peeled and segmented, to garnish

CREAMY AVOCADO VINAIGRETTE
1 avocado, halved, pitted, peeled, and diced
2 tablespoons fresh lemon juice
2 tablespoons chopped fresh cilantro
1 jalapeño pepper, stemmed, seeded, and chopped
2 cups water
1 teaspoon sea salt

Trim and discard the stems and remove all the leaves of the artichokes. Cut them in half and remove the furry centers. Steam the artichoke hearts until just tender, 30 minutes, remove from the steamer, and let cool. Cut into quarters and set aside.

To make the dressing, combine the avocado, lemon juice, cilantro, jalapeño pepper, water, and salt in a blender and blend until smooth. Taste and adjust the seasonings, if necessary.

In a large bowl, gently toss the artichokes, hearts of palm, mâche, and endive together. Add the dressing and toss again.

To serve, arrange the salad on individual salad plates and garnish with the orange segments.

ROSEMARY PORTOBELLO STEAKS with CELERIAC PUREE, CABERNET REDUCTION, and BRUSSELS SPROUTS

This is a very impressive dish that pulls out all the stops for Valentine's Day. Rich and meaty portobello mushrooms marinated in olive oil and fresh herbs are the centerpiece of this deeply satisfying dish. They're served over a smooth celeriac puree with sautéed brussels sprouts, ruby red cranberries, and a reduction of Cabernet.

SERVES 4 TO 6

CELERIAC PUREE
2 pounds celeriac, peeled and diced
2 white onions, sliced
3 tablespoons Earth Balance Natural Buttery Spread
½ teaspoon sea salt

PORTOBELLO STEAKS
6 large portobello mushrooms, stemmed and thinly sliced
1 tablespoon sea salt
1 teaspoon freshly ground black pepper
2 tablespoons chopped fresh rosemary
1 tablespoon chopped fresh flat-leaf parsley
½ cup extra-virgin olive oil

CABERNET REDUCTION
½ (750 ml) bottle Cabernet
2 bay leaves
⅓ cup unrefined sugar

BRUSSELS SPROUTS
1 pound brussels sprouts, trimmed and halved
1 tablespoon extra-virgin olive oil
Sea salt and freshly ground black pepper
½ cup dried cranberries

To make the celeriac puree, bring 3 quarts of water to a boil in a large pot. Add the celeriac and onions and cook until the celeriac is soft, 30 to 40 minutes. Drain and let cool.

Transfer the onions and celeriac to a large bowl. Add the buttery spread and salt and mix together. Transfer the mixture to a food processor and blend until smooth.

Meanwhile, to make the portobello steaks, put the mushrooms in a large bowl and add the salt, pepper, rosemary, parsley, and olive oil. Gently mix all the ingredients together with your hands and let sit for up to 1 hour.

Heat a large sauté pan over medium-high heat, add half of the mushrooms, and cook, stirring occasionally, until tender, 5 to 8 minutes. Remove with a slotted spoon and repeat with the remaining mushrooms.

To make the reduction, combine the wine, bay leaves, and sugar in a small saucepan. Cook over high heat for 20 minutes, until the wine is reduced by half. Remove the bay leaves and cook for an additional 15 to 20 minutes, until the reduction becomes a syrup. Set aside. Reheat before serving, if necessary.

To prepare the brussels sprouts, bring 2 quarts of water to a boil in a large pot. Add the brussels sprouts and cook until they lose their dark green color and begin to soften, about 5 minutes. Drain and let cool for 5 minutes.

Heat the oil over medium-high heat in a large sauté pan. Add the sprouts and salt and pepper to taste and cook, stirring occasionally, until golden brown, 5 to 10 minutes. Add the cranberries and cook until the berries start to soften, about 2 minutes.

To serve, spoon the puree in the center of an individual serving plate, add the brussels sprouts, top with the mushrooms, and drizzle with the wine reduction. Any leftovers will keep in the refrigerator for up to 4 days.

MOREL-CRUSTED TOFU with SAUTÉED MUSHROOMS and FENNEL and POMEGRANATE SALAD

We love the rich and robust flavor of this dish made with marinated tofu and mushrooms. Morel powder, made from wild morel mushrooms, adds a deep, earthy flavor to a variety of dishes, and it is available in gourmet shops and online. You can also make your own by grinding dried morels or wild mushrooms in a coffee or spice grinder. This delectable dish is topped with a salad of fresh fennel and ruby red pomegranate seeds that add just the right color and zest to your Valentine's dinner.

SERVES 4

2 (14-ounce) blocks extra-firm tofu
4 tablespoons extra-virgin olive oil
2 tablespoons fresh lemon juice
1 tablespoon stone-ground mustard
Sea salt and freshly ground black pepper
1 cup unbleached all-purpose flour
1 tablespoon morel powder
Sea salt and freshly ground black pepper
½ cup extra-virgin olive oil

2 tablespoons Earth Balance Natural Buttery Spread
2 pounds mixed mushrooms, such as portobello, cremini, oyster, and chanterelle, stemmed and cut into small pieces
1 tablespoon chopped fresh chives
1 teaspoon chopped fresh oregano
2 teaspoons chopped fresh flat-leaf parsley
2 bulbs fennel, trimmed and thinly sliced
1 cup pomegranate seeds
2 tablespoons fresh lemon juice
1 tablespoon finely grated lemon zest

Drain and slice each block of tofu crosswise into 4 pieces. Remove excess water from the tofu by squeezing with paper towels. Transfer to a large bowl.

Whisk together the olive oil, lemon juice, mustard, and salt and pepper to taste. Pour over the tofu and toss to coat. Cover and let marinate in the refrigerator for 4 hours, or overnight.

Combine the flour, morel powder, and salt and pepper to taste in a large bowl and toss together. Dredge the tofu pieces to coat evenly and set aside.

Heat the olive oil in a large sauté pan over medium-low heat. When the oil is hot, fry the tofu until golden brown, 2 to 3 minutes per side. Transfer the tofu to a plate lined with paper towels.

Heat another sauté pan over medium heat and melt the buttery spread. Add the mushrooms, chives, oregano, and 1 teaspoon of the parsley and cook, stirring occasionally, until the water has drained out of the mushrooms, 10 to 15 minutes. Add additional salt and pepper to taste.

Combine the fennel and pomegranate seeds in a large bowl and toss together. Add the lemon juice, lemon zest, the remaining teaspoon of parsley, and additional salt and pepper to taste.

To serve, put 2 pieces of tofu on each plate. Spoon the mushroom mixture over the tofu and top with the fennel and pomegranate salad. Any leftovers will keep in the refrigerator for up to 4 days.

PASSION FRUIT CRÈME BRÛLÉE

We serve creamy crème brûlée for all sorts of special occasions. It's fantastic with passion fruit puree and many other flavors, such as lemon, mango, and papaya. This light and sweet dessert is a delectable way to say I love you.

SERVES 6

1 (13.5-ounce) can coconut milk
½ cup soy creamer
¼ cup coconut sugar
2 ¼ teaspoons agar powder
¾ cup passion fruit puree
¼ cup unrefined sugar

Combine the coconut milk, soy creamer, coconut sugar, and agar in a large saucepan and bring to a boil over medium heat. Remove from the heat and set aside to cool.

Oil 6 (4-inch) ramekins.

After the coconut mixture has cooled, stir in the passion fruit puree, pour the mixture into the ramekins, and refrigerate for 30 minutes. (At this point, any extra crème brûlées can be refrigerated for serving the following day.)

Remove the ramekins from the refrigerator and put them on a rack or a foil-lined baking sheet. Sprinkle 1 tablespoon of the unrefined sugar evenly on the top of each ramekin. With a kitchen butane torch, carefully heat the sugar evenly to form a hard sugar topping. Serve at once.

MOLTEN CHOCOLATE CAKE with RASPBERRY COULIS

────

What is Valentine's Day without chocolate? These simple, elegant mini cakes served with raspberry coulis are a perfect ending to this sumptuous meal.

SERVES 6

RASPBERRY COULIS
3 cups fresh or frozen raspberries, thawed if frozen
1 cup unrefined sugar
2 cups water

2/3 cup plain unsweetened soy milk
1/2 cup safflower oil
1/4 cup maple syrup
2 tablespoons unrefined sugar
1/4 teaspoon apple cider vinegar
1/2 cup unbleached all-purpose flour
1/4 cup natural cocoa powder
1 1/2 teaspoons baking powder
1/4 teaspoon baking soda
Pinch of sea salt
3/4 cup vegan semisweet chocolate chips

Confectioners' sugar, to dust

To prepare the coulis, combine the raspberries, sugar, and water in a medium saucepan and simmer over medium-low heat, stirring occasionally, for 20 minutes. Remove from the heat and let cool. Transfer to a blender and blend until smooth. Strain the mixture into a bowl and let cool in the refrigerator until you are ready to serve.

Meanwhile, preheat the oven to 350°F. Oil 6 cups of a standard muffin tin.

Combine 1/2 cup of the soy milk, the oil, maple syrup, sugar, and vinegar in a large bowl and beat with an electric mixer fitted with the whisk attachment at medium speed until smooth. Add the flour and cocoa powder and beat until incorporated, 3 to 5 minutes. Add the remaining soy milk, the baking powder, baking soda, and salt and beat until incorporated.

Divide the batter among the prepared muffin cups so they are all three-quarters full. Put 2 tablespoons of chocolate chips into the center of each cake and gently press them down with your fingers, until they are covered by the batter. Bake for about 20 minutes, until the batter is puffed but the center is not set.

To serve, flip the muffin pan upside down onto a board to unmold the cakes. Transfer the cakes to dessert plates, dust with confectioners' sugar, and drizzle with the raspberry coulis. Serve warm. Any leftovers will keep in the refrigerator for up to 4 days.

PASSOVER SEDER

A seder is a ritual feast that marks the beginning of Passover and, because it usually falls in late March or early April, it is also a celebration of the coming of spring. Joy grew up with her family hosting seders, and she continues the tradition today by bringing generations of her family and friends to the table. She has taken a number of traditional Passover recipes, such as chopped liver, gefilte fish, and brisket, and transformed them into plant-based vegan dishes that are amazingly satisfying and delicious. And as an added bonus, many of them can be made well ahead of time.

CONCORD GRAPE SODA

This soda is a very refreshing drink for a seder. Grape juice is considered an unleavened wine and is popular on many seder tables, including ours. It is a little sweet and tart and pairs well with our favorite Passover dishes.

SERVES 1

2 ounces Concord grape juice
1 ounce fresh lemon juice
½ ounce agave nectar
Ice
Sparkling water
3 pinches of cayenne pepper
1 large purple grape, to garnish

Pour the grape juice, lemon juice, and agave into a highball glass. Add ice, top with sparkling water, and stir. Sprinkle with cayenne pepper. Split the grape halfway through, set on the rim of the glass, and serve.

HAROSET

The tradition of eating haroset during the Passover seder dates back at least 1500 years. There are other versions of this dish—some are made with dried fruit only, some omit the wine. Ours is a sweet apple-based one. Be sure to use firm, tart apples like Granny Smiths and to make it on the same day you are serving it so it retains its crunch.

SERVES 8 TO 10

4 Granny Smith apples, peeled, cored, and finely diced
½ cup raisins
½ cup golden raisins
½ cup walnuts, chopped
¼ cup fresh orange juice
¼ cup red wine
2 tablespoons agave nectar
½ teaspoon ground cinnamon
1 (11-ounce) package matzo

Combine the apples, raisins, walnuts, orange juice, wine, agave, and cinnamon in a bowl and mix together. Cover and refrigerate for 2 hours before serving.

Serve the haroset in a large serving bowl or two smaller ones, one at each end of the table, with matzo passed around on the side.

CHOPPED "LIVER"

Although this recipe is fairly labor-intensive, it is well worth the work. You may want to double the recipe since it disappears quickly from the table, and you may want to keep some for delicious leftovers. It is also best to make it the day before you're planning to serve it to let the flavors blend and intensify. Serve this fantastic spread with matzo or crudités.

SERVES 8 TO 10

¼ cup walnuts
1 cup dried chickpeas, covered with water and soaked
 overnight in the refrigerator
1 bay leaf
3 tablespoons extra-virgin olive oil
6 portobello mushrooms, stemmed, peeled, and finely diced
1 white onion, finely diced
1 tablespoon sea salt, plus more if needed
½ teaspoon freshly ground black pepper, plus more
 if needed

Preheat the oven to 350°F.

Spread out the walnuts on a baking sheet and roast them for about 5 minutes, until lightly browned. Remove from the oven and let cool. Peel the walnuts and set aside.

Bring 4 cups of water to a boil in a large pot. Drain the chickpeas and add to the pot with the bay leaf. Cook uncovered over high heat until tender, about 45 minutes. Drain, remove the bay leaf, and let cool.

Heat 1 tablespoon of the olive oil in a large sauté pan over medium heat. Add the mushrooms and cook for 20 minutes. Drain and set aside.

In another sauté pan, heat 1 tablespoon of the olive oil over medium heat. Add the onion, decrease the heat, and cook over medium-low heat until caramelized, about 30 minutes. Remove from the heat and let cool.

Transfer the walnuts, chickpeas, mushrooms, onion, the remaining 1 tablespoon of olive oil, salt, and pepper to a blender and blend until smooth. Taste and adjust the seasonings, if necessary. The chopped liver will keep, covered, in the refrigerator for up to 2 days before serving. Serve in a bowl at room temperature.

GEFILTE TOFU with FRESH HORSERADISH and BEET RELISH

Gefilte fish is a traditional seder appetizer that is made with ground whitefish and matzo meal. We created a very tasty vegan version that is made with firm and silken tofu, carrots, and celery. The taste and the texture are spot on! Note that if you don't have a juicer to make the beet juice, you can substitute an extra half cup of finely shredded beets.

SERVES 8 TO 10

1 (14-ounce) block extra-firm tofu
8 ounces silken tofu
2 teaspoons extra-virgin olive oil
¼ cup finely chopped carrot
¼ cup finely chopped celery
½ teaspoon finely chopped garlic
2 tablespoons finely chopped shallots
1 teaspoon sea salt
1 teaspoon agar powder

HORSERADISH & BEET RELISH

1½ cups finely shredded fresh horseradish
½ cup finely shredded fresh raw beets
¼ cup beet juice
1 teaspoon white wine vinegar
1 teaspoon sea salt

Minced fresh chives, to garnish

To make the gefilte tofu, cut the firm tofu in half and finely chop one-half of it.

Put the silken tofu in a large bowl. Take the whole piece of extra-firm tofu and crumble it into the bowl. Add the chopped extra-firm tofu to the bowl, toss the different tofus together, and set aside.

Heat the olive oil in a large sauté pan over medium heat. Add the carrot, celery, garlic, shallots, and salt and cook until softened, 3 to 5 minutes. Add the reserved tofu and agar to the pan and cook, stirring constantly to prevent sticking, for 10 minutes. Remove from the heat and let cool for 5 minutes.

Using a tablespoon or a small ice cream scoop, form the tofu into balls, put them on a baking sheet, and let sit for 30 minutes. The tofu will keep in the refrigerator, covered with plastic wrap, for up to 2 days.

To make the relish, combine the horseradish, beets, beet juice, vinegar, and salt in a bowl.

To serve, put a scoop of the gefilte tofu on a salad plate, spoon the relish on the side, and garnish with fresh chives.

LEMONGRASS-INFUSED CELERIAC SOUP with MATZO BALLS

Matzo ball soup is classic comfort food. A steaming bowl of it on a winter day (or any day) is always the right thing to eat. Our vegan version is made with onions, carrots, and celeriac (or celery root), and we add a stalk of lemongrass to impart a lively citrus flavor to the soup. Both the soup and matzo balls can be made ahead of time. For matzo balls, let cool to room temperature after removing from the water and store, covered, on a tray in the refrigerator. Steam to reheat before serving.

SERVES 8 TO 10; MAKES ABOUT 20 MATZO BALLS

3 tablespoons extra-virgin olive oil
1 stalk lemongrass, cut into 4 pieces
2 cups trimmed, peeled, and diced celeriac
1 cup diced white onion
1 cup diced carrots
2 cups sliced baby cremini mushrooms
8 cups vegetable stock
¼ teaspoon chopped fresh oregano
¼ teaspoon chopped fresh thyme
½ teaspoon sea salt
½ teaspoon freshly ground black pepper

MATZO BALLS
1 cup matzo meal
1 teaspoon baking powder
¼ teaspoon sea salt
¼ teaspoon garlic powder
¼ teaspoon onion powder
¼ teaspoon freshly ground black pepper
½ cup sparkling water
2 tablespoons grapeseed oil
1 small potato, peeled, steamed, and mashed
1 tablespoon chopped fresh flat-leaf parsley

To make the soup, heat the olive oil in a soup pot over medium-high heat. Add the lemongrass, celeriac, onion, carrots, and mushrooms and cook for 5 minutes. Add the vegetable stock, oregano, thyme, and salt and pepper and simmer over medium heat until the vegetables are tender, 20 to 30 minutes. Taste and adjust the seasonings, if necessary, and discard the lemongrass. Keep warm on the stove. The soup can be made ahead of time and will keep, covered, in the refrigerator, for up to 3 days, or in the freezer for up to 1 month. Reheat before serving.

To make the matzo balls, combine the matzo meal, baking powder, salt, garlic powder, onion powder, and pepper in a small bowl and mix together with a fork.

Combine the sparkling water, grapeseed oil, and mashed potato in another bowl and mix together.

Add the potato mixture to the dry ingredients and add the parsley. Mix all of the ingredients together with a fork until just combined. Do not overmix.

With your hands, form the matzo mixture into ¾-inch balls and arrange on a large plate or baking sheet. Put them in the refrigerator and let rest until firm and chilled, 20 to 30 minutes.

Bring 3 quarts of water to a boil in a large soup pot over medium-high heat. Decrease the heat to a simmer and drop the matzo balls gently into the water. Cover and simmer until soft and fluffy, 30 to 35 minutes.

Using a slotted spoon, remove the matzo balls from the water, spoon 2 into each soup bowl and pour the soup over them. Serve immediately.

SWEET POTATO and APRICOT TZIMMES

Tzimmes is a traditional side dish served at Passover and Hanukkah, usually made with carrots, sweet potatoes, and dried fruit. Here we simmer and bake it with fresh apricots and orange juice to give it a lighter flavor. If you can't find fresh apricots, use dried.

SERVES 8 TO 10

6 carrots, peeled and diced
4 sweet potatoes, peeled and diced
2 cups quartered fresh or dried apricots
2 teaspoons fresh lemon juice
½ cup fresh orange juice
⅔ cup maple syrup
2 teaspoons ground cinnamon
2 teaspoons finely grated orange zest
1 teaspoon freshly grated nutmeg
Pinch of sea salt

Preheat the oven to 350°F. Oil a large baking dish.

Bring 10 cups of water to a boil in a large pot. Add the carrots and sweet potatoes and cook for 10 minutes. Drain.

Transfer the carrots and sweet potatoes to a large bowl. Add the apricots, lemon juice, orange juice, maple syrup, cinnamon, orange zest, nutmeg, and salt and stir together to mix well.

Put the mixture in the prepared baking dish and bake for 15 minutes. Remove from the oven, stir, and continue baking until the carrots and potatoes are tender, about 15 minutes.

Remove the tzimmes from the oven and serve.

SWISS CHARD & CHICKPEAS

This is a favorite dish that originated with Lottie Bildirici, a member of our extended Candle family. In addition to being one of our recipe testers and chef's assistants in cooking classes, she's a very talented home cook. Hearty greens and beans, like Swiss chard and chickpeas, are a naturally good combination, and all types of chard—red, yellow, or rainbow—work really well in this recipe.

SERVES 8 TO 10

2 tablespoons extra-virgin olive oil
2 small yellow onions, diced
1 jalapeño pepper, stemmed, seeded, and chopped
2 cloves garlic, minced
1 fresh thyme leaf, chopped
1 cup peeled and diced fresh tomatoes
½ cup red wine
2 bunches Swiss chard, stemmed and leaves
    coarsely chopped
1 cup cooked or 1 (15-ounce) can chickpeas, rinsed
    and drained
Sea salt and freshly ground black pepper

Heat the olive oil in a large skillet over medium-high heat. Add the onions and jalapeño and sauté until softened, about 5 minutes.

Add the garlic, thyme, and tomatoes. Decrease the heat and cook, stirring occasionally, until softened, 3 to 5 minutes.

Add the wine and bring to a simmer. Add the Swiss chard and toss with tongs until coated. Cook, tossing well, until it is tender and just wilted, 2 or 3 minutes. Add the chickpeas and simmer until they are warmed through, 3 to 5 minutes.

Add salt and pepper to taste and serve immediately.

SWEET POTATO LATKES with ALMOND CRÈME FRAÎCHE

Who doesn't love latkes? Although we always serve them for Passover, we also make them year-round, as party appetizers and a side dish. Our crispy pancakes are made with a mix of russets, sweet potatoes, and fresh chives, and we top them with a dollop of creamy almond crème fraîche. To ensure that your latkes are crisp, be sure to squeeze out as much water as possible from the shredded potatoes before you add them to the other ingredients. Note that the almonds are soaked overnight.

SERVES 8 TO 10; MAKES ABOUT 24 PANCAKES

ALMOND CRÈME FRAÎCHE
2 cups sliced almonds
2 tablespoons fresh lemon juice
3 tablespoons canola oil
½ cup water
1½ teaspoons sea salt

1 pound russet potatoes, peeled and rinsed
1 pound sweet potatoes, peeled and rinsed
½ teaspoon sea salt
½ teaspoon freshly ground black pepper
3 tablespoons extra-virgin olive oil
1 white onion, finely chopped
3 tablespoons chopped fresh chives
1 cup dried bread crumbs
¼ cup Earth Balance Natural Buttery Spread
   or extra-virgin olive oil, plus more as needed

To make the crème fraîche, put the almonds in a large bowl and cover with at least 2 inches of water. Let soak overnight. Rinse and drain the almonds.

Transfer the almonds to a food processor. Add the lemon juice, canola oil, water, and salt. Blend until smooth, 8 to 10 minutes. Transfer to a bowl and refrigerate for 1 hour. The crème fraîche will keep, covered, in the refrigerator for up to 2 days.

Using a box grater or a food processor, grate the potatoes and put them in a large bowl. Add the salt and pepper and mix together. With a clean kitchen towel, squeeze the excess liquid from the potatoes and return them to the bowl.

Heat the olive oil in a sauté pan over medium heat. Add the onion and sauté until softened, 5 to 8 minutes. Add 2 tablespoons of the chives and the bread crumbs to the potatoes and mix together. With your hands, form the mixture into patties that are about 3 inches wide and ½ inch thick and place on parchment paper.

Heat the buttery spread in a nonstick skillet over medium-low heat. Cook the latkes until lightly browned and crisp, about 4 minutes per side. Add more buttery spread, if needed. Remove latkes from the pan with a spatula and let drain on paper towels. Note: If you prefer to bake the latkes, bake them in a 350°F oven on an oiled baking sheet for 20 minutes, 10 minutes per side.

Serve the latkes with crème fraîche and garnish with the remaining 1 tablespoon of chives.

JOY'S GRANDMA'S SEITAN BRISKET with ROASTED CARROTS, SHALLOTS, and TURNIPS

This wonderful one-pot dish of seitan and vegetables is the centerpiece of the seder, and it will fill your kitchen with aromas of holidays past. Look for baby carrots, turnips, and fingerling potatoes at farmers' markets because the season for them is just right. This recipe was lovingly handed down to Joy from her grandmother Minerva, and she continues her delicious family tradition, vegan-style.

SERVES 8 TO 10

2 tablespoons unbleached all-purpose flour
2 pounds seitan, in 1 or 2 large pieces
1½ teaspoons sea salt
1½ teaspoons freshly ground black pepper
1½ teaspoons smoked paprika
2 tablespoons extra-virgin olive oil
1 Vidalia onion, coarsely chopped
½ cup red wine
2 tablespoons white wine vinegar
1 tablespoon tamari
3 cups peeled and diced plum tomatoes
½ teaspoon chopped fresh flat-leaf parsley
½ teaspoon chopped fresh chives
¼ teaspoon chopped fresh rosemary leaves
¼ teaspoon chopped fresh oregano
2 bunches baby carrots, trimmed and peeled
2 bunches baby turnips, trimmed and peeled
1 pound fingerling potatoes, halved
1 pound shallots, peeled and halved

Preheat the oven to 350°F.

Put the flour in a shallow bowl and dredge the seitan to coat completely. Sprinkle the seitan with the salt, pepper, and paprika. Heat 1 tablespoon of the olive oil over medium-high heat in a large sauté pan and brown the seitan on all sides, about 6 minutes. Remove the seitan from the pan and set aside.

Add the remaining 1 tablespoon of the olive oil to the pan, add the onion, and cook over medium heat, scraping up the browned bits, until softened, about 5 minutes. Add the wine, vinegar, and tamari, and cook, stirring until the sauce begins to thicken, 3 to 5 minutes. Add the tomatoes, parsley, chives, rosemary, and oregano and cook, stirring occasionally to break up the tomatoes, until the sauce is thickened, 15 to 20 minutes.

Combine the seitan, carrots, turnips, potatoes, and shallots in a large roasting pan and pour the tomato sauce over them. Cover the pan with aluminum foil and roast for 45 minutes. Remove the foil and roast until the vegetables are fork-tender, about 15 minutes.

Slice the seitan and serve with the vegetables and juices.

CHICKPEA CREPES with BERRIES and VANILLA-LAVENDER CREAM

Although we usually think of crepes made with chickpea flour as a savory dish, they also work beautifully as a dessert. In this recipe we fill them with fresh berries and luscious vanilla-lavender cream. Dried lavender can be found in the spice section of markets and online.

SERVES 8 TO 10

1 cup plain unsweetened soy milk
½ cup chickpea flour
½ cup arrowroot powder
¼ cup unrefined sugar
⅛ teaspoon vanilla extract
Pinch of sea salt

VANILLA-LAVENDER CREAM
1 cup coconut milk
1 tablespoon dried lavender flowers
2 cups confectioners' sugar
1 teaspoon vanilla extract

4 cups fresh berries, such as strawberries, blueberries, and blackberries
½ cup confectioners' sugar, to serve

To make the crepes, combine the soy milk, chickpea flour, arrowroot powder, sugar, vanilla, and salt in a blender and blend until smooth.

Spray a nonstick skillet or crepe pan with cooking spray, heat the pan over medium heat, and then pour about ¼ cup of the batter into the center of the pan. Quickly lift the pan off the heat and tip it in several directions so the batter covers the bottom of the pan.

Return the pan to the heat and cook for 2 to 3 minutes, or until the edges of the crepe begin to brown. Using a spatula, flip the crepe and cook for about 1 minute, until lightly browned. Transfer the crepe to a plate. Continue cooking crepes with the remaining batter, adding more cooking spray if needed, and stacking the crepes on top of each other as they are cooked.

To make the cream, combine the coconut milk, lavender flowers, confectioners' sugar, and vanilla in a blender and blend until a smooth liquid forms, about 5 minutes. Strain the mixture into a bowl through a chinois.

To serve, arrange a crepe in the center of each plate. Spoon berries onto half of the crepe and add a dollop of the lavender cream on top of the fruit. Fold the crepe over the fruit and cream. Dust with confectioners' sugar, garnish with additional berries, and serve.

FLOURLESS CHOCOLATE CAKE with MACAROON CRUST

Since it is traditional not to eat wheat flour or any leavening agents during the Passover season, baking for the holiday has always been a bit of a challenge. We got it right with this dense, delicious chocolate cake. When making the macaroon crust, be sure that the carrots are thoroughly dry before using them.

SERVES 8 TO 10

MACAROON CRUST
½ cup shredded carrots, drained and patted dry
½ cup unsweetened coconut flakes
½ cup sliced almonds
½ cup maple syrup
1 tablespoon Ener-G egg replacer
¼ cup brown rice syrup
½ cup water

2 cups almond meal
½ cup natural cocoa powder
2 tablespoons baking powder
1 tablespoon ground cinnamon
1 cup plain unsweetened soy milk
½ cup maple syrup
1 teaspoon apple cider vinegar
1 cup safflower oil
½ cup unrefined sugar

Confectioners' sugar, for dusting

Preheat the oven to 350°F. Oil a 10-inch cake pan.

To make the crust, combine the carrots, coconut flakes, almonds, maple syrup, egg replacer, brown rice syrup, and water in a large bowl and mix together thoroughly. Transfer the mixture to the prepared pan and, pressing with your hands, form an even crust along the bottom and partially up the sides of the pan. Bake until lightly browned, about 10 minutes. Remove from the oven and set aside.

To make the cake, combine the almond meal, cocoa powder, baking powder, and cinnamon in a large bowl and mix together thoroughly.

Combine the soy milk, maple syrup, apple cider vinegar, oil, and sugar in a blender and blend for 2 minutes. Add to the dry ingredients and mix together until well blended.

Pour the mixture evenly onto the crust in the pan. Bake for 20 to 30 minutes, until the top of the cake is crisp.

To serve, dust the cake with confectioners' sugar and cut into wedges.

EASTER BRUNCH

Easter is a harbinger of springtime and yet another wonderful holiday for feasting with family and friends. It is a great time to seek out fresh vegetables like asparagus, fava beans, and fresh peas at the market and prepare lighter fare, such as spring salads and artichokes. Over Easter weekend, we prepare a festive brunch that features salads, quinoa vegetable cakes, pineapple-glazed seitan, and eye-opening cocktails and then bring everyone to our big table, which is decorated with bunches of daffodils, baskets of fresh-baked muffins, and jars of homemade preserves. Welcome spring!

CANDLE ROYALE

In our twist on the popular kir royale, we make cassis pearls with agar and cassis liqueur. Agar powder is a vegetarian gelatin that is derived from seaweed. It is widely available in health food stores, Asian markets, and online. The sweet pearls are a beautiful garnish and enhance the flavors of sparkling white wine and elderflower liqueur.

SERVES 1

CASSIS PEARLS
1½ cups extra-virgin olive oil
3 ounces cassis liqueur
¼ teaspoon agar powder

5 ounces sparkling white wine
1 ounce elderflower liqueur

To make the pearls, put the olive oil in the freezer for at least 30 minutes or up to 1 hour. The oil has to be cold in order for the pearls to form.

Mix together the cassis liqueur and agar in a saucepan and bring to a boil over medium-high heat. Pour into a bowl and let it cool for 2 minutes.

Pour the chilled olive oil into a pint glass. Using a dropper or a squeeze bottle, drip the cassis mixture into the cold oil. Once the pearls are formed, remove them from the oil with a scoop and rinse them gently with cold water. (The oil can be reused.)

Combine the wine and elderflower liqueur in a champagne flute and drop in a half-teaspoon of cassis pearls. The pearls will sink and dissolve slowly.

AÇAI MIMOSA

Every brunch party should include mimosas, and one of our favorites is made with açai liqueur and sparkling rosé. It has a deeper, fruitier flavor than a traditional mimosa.

SERVES 1

5 ounces sparkling rosé
1 ounce VeeV açai spirit
1 sprig thyme
Orange slice, to garnish

Pour the rosé and the liqueur into a champagne flute and stir well. Top with the thyme sprig, garnish with the orange slice, and serve.

FAIR MARY

The Candle Bloody Mary has a good spicy kick of Sriracha sauce and is a very popular eye-opener at our weekend brunches in our restaurants, as well as at our parties. We prefer to use Fair Quinoa Vodka, known for its herbal quality, for this particular cocktail.

SERVES 1

1½ ounces vodka
2 ounces tomato juice
½ ounce fresh lemon juice
1 teaspoon fresh thyme leaves
¼ teaspoon freshly peeled and grated horseradish
Dash of Sriracha sauce
Sea salt and freshly ground black pepper
Ice
3 large Spanish olives, to garnish

Combine the vodka, tomato juice, lemon juice, and thyme leaves in a cocktail shaker. Add the horseradish, Sriracha, salt and pepper to taste, and ice and shake well. Pour into a rocks glass filled with ice, thread the olives onto a skewer to garnish, and serve.

MINI MUFFINS with HOMEMADE PRESERVES

These tasty little muffins bring everyone to the table, especially kids. We like to add in fresh berries, pineapple, or nuts to the batter and serve them with a selection of homemade preserves. The possibilities are endless.

MAKES ABOUT 2 DOZEN MUFFINS

HOMEMADE PRESERVES

2 cups coarsely chopped fresh Concord grapes, peaches, strawberries, figs, or blueberries

½ cup unrefined sugar

1 teaspoon agar powder

2 cups unbleached all-purpose flour

¼ cup unrefined sugar

1 teaspoon baking powder

½ teaspoon baking soda

¼ teaspoon sea salt

½ cup Earth Balance Natural Buttery Spread, melted

½ cup maple syrup

½ cup plain unsweetened soy milk

½ cup fresh raspberries, cranberries, diced pineapple, mashed banana, chopped nuts, or 2 teaspoons ground cinnamon

Chocolate chips, nuts, toasted coconut (optional)

To make the preserves, combine the fruit, sugar, and agar in a saucepan and stir. Cook over medium heat until the mixture thickens, 20 to 30 minutes. Remove from the heat and let cool for 30 minutes.

Preheat the oven to 350°F. Oil a 24-cup mini-muffin tin.

To make the muffins, in a large bowl, whisk together the flour, sugar, baking powder, baking soda, and salt.

In another bowl, mix together the buttery spread, maple syrup, and soy milk.

Add the wet ingredients to the dry ingredients and whisk until just combined, being careful not to overmix. Stir in the fruit. Spoon the batter into the muffin tins, filling each cup about two-thirds full.

Top the batter with chips, nuts, toasted coconut, or any other items of your choosing. Bake for about 10 minutes, until golden brown.

Remove the muffins from the pan and let cool on a plate before serving with the preserves.

FRENCH TOAST COFFEE CAKE

Here is an incredibly moist coffee cake with a lovely texture of layered sourdough bread and a crumble of coconut sugar and cinnamon. The cake can be made a day or two ahead of time, and any leftovers will go well with the following morning's coffee.

SERVES 8 TO 10

1 cup vegan cream cheese
3 cups plain unsweetened soy milk
3 tablespoons unrefined sugar
1 tablespoon Ener-G egg replacer
1½ tablespoons fresh ginger juice
1 tablespoon ground cinnamon
8 slices sourdough bread, cut into 1- to 2-inch rounds
¼ cup coconut sugar
1 tablespoon ground cinnamon
2 tablespoons Earth Balance Natural Buttery Spread, melted
2 tablespoons unbleached all-purpose flour
Maple syrup, fresh fruit, and berries, to serve

Preheat the oven to 400°F. Oil a 9-inch springform pan and wrap the base of the pan in aluminum foil to prevent leaking.

Combine the cream cheese, soy milk, sugar, egg replacer, ginger juice, and cinnamon in a blender and blend for 5 minutes. Transfer the mixture to a large shallow dish, add the bread, and let sit it for 5 minutes, turning the bread pieces occasionally.

In a bowl, combine the coconut sugar, cinnamon, buttery spread, and flour and mix until it has a crumby consistency.

Put half of the bread and cream cheese mixture in the prepared pan and top with half of the cinnamon-sugar mixture. Repeat with the remaining bread, cream cheese mixture, and cinnamon-sugar mixture.

Bake the coffee cake for about 45 minutes, until golden brown and a cake tester comes out clean. Let it cool in the pan for 15 minutes.

Unmold the coffee cake, cut into wedges, and serve with maple syrup and fresh fruit, if desired.

SPRING VEGETABLE SALAD with FAVA BEANS, PEAS, ASPARAGUS, and LEMON-CHIVE DRESSING

This salad is full of springtime treats—fresh fava beans, peas, and asparagus. While preparing them may be rather labor-intensive, the delicious results are well worth it when they're tossed together with lively lemon-chive dressing and tender baby greens. This is seasonal eating at its best.

SERVES 8 TO 10

2 cups fresh or frozen fava beans, rinsed
2 cups fresh or frozen English peas
2 bunches fresh asparagus, trimmed, cut into 1-inch
   pieces and halved lengthwise

LEMON-CHIVE DRESSING
1 cup grapeseed oil
⅓ cup fresh lemon juice
½ cup chopped fresh chives
1 tablespoon chopped fresh tarragon
1½ teaspoons sea salt
½ teaspoon black pepper

1 pound baby greens
½ cup roasted sunflower seeds

Bring 4 quarts of water to a boil in a large pot. Decrease the heat, add the fava beans, and simmer for 2 minutes. Add the peas and asparagus and simmer until all of the vegetables are tender, 4 to 6 minutes. Drain and transfer to a bowl of cold water.

Peel the outer skins of the fava beans and rinse with cold water. Drain the vegetables again and transfer to a large bowl.

To make the dressing, put the oil, lemon juice, chives, tarragon, salt, and pepper in a blender and blend until smooth. Taste and adjust the seasonings, if necessary.

Add the greens to the vegetables and toss with some of the dressing. Drizzle with additional dressing, sprinkle with sunflower seeds, and serve.

GRILLED ARTICHOKE HEARTS with PESTO

We love to play around with pesto, and this version is full of fresh herbs—parsley, basil, and chives—and some nutritional yeast that adds a cheeselike flavor. It tastes terrific with fresh springtime artichokes.

SERVES 8 TO 10

5 artichokes
2 tablespoons extra-virgin olive oil
Sea salt and freshly ground black pepper

PESTO
½ cup pine nuts
½ cup cashews
1 tablespoon fresh lemon juice
1 tablespoon nutritional yeast
⅓ cup extra-virgin olive oil
1 cup chopped fresh flat-leaf parsley
1 cup fresh basil leaves
½ cup chopped fresh chives
Sea salt and freshly ground black pepper

Preheat the oven to 350°F.

Trim and discard the stems and remove all the leaves of the artichokes. Cut them in half and remove the furry centers.

Put the artichokes on a baking sheet and toss them with the olive oil and salt and pepper to taste. Cover with aluminum foil and bake for 25 to 35 minutes, until fork-tender. Set aside.

To make the pesto, combine the pine nuts, cashews, lemon juice, nutritional yeast, and olive oil in a food processor and blend until smooth. Add the parsley, basil, and chives and blend again until smooth. Add salt and pepper to taste.

Heat an oiled grill or grill pan over medium heat and grill the artichokes until lightly browned, 2 to 3 minutes per side.

Arrange the artichokes on a platter, spoon a dollop of pesto onto each half, and serve.

QUINOA VEGETABLE CAKES

These savory cakes are a perfect accompaniment to Pineapple-Ginger Glazed Seitan (page 72) or any other seitan dish. They are well seasoned and hold their shape beautifully. When served with a spring salad, they also make a healthy, delicious lunch or light dinner.

SERVES 8 TO 10

4 cups water
3 bay leaves
2 cups quinoa, rinsed and drained
3 tablespoons extra-virgin olive oil
1 cup diced yellow onions
1 cup peeled and diced carrots
½ cup diced celery
½ cup seeded and diced red bell pepper
½ cup dried bread crumbs
1 tablespoon chopped fresh cilantro
½ teaspoon sea salt
½ teaspoon freshly ground black pepper

Bring the water and bay leaves to a boil in a large pot. Add the quinoa, decrease the heat to a simmer, and cook, covered, for 15 to 20 minutes. Remove the bay leaves and set aside the quinoa to cool.

Heat the olive oil in a large sauté pan over medium-high heat. Add the onions and cook until caramelized, about 5 minutes. Add the carrots, celery, and red pepper and cook for an additional 5 minutes. Remove from the heat and set aside.

Preheat the oven to 350°F. Oil a baking sheet.

In a large bowl, mix the quinoa and vegetables together. Transfer half of the mixture to a food processor and blend until smooth. Return it to the bowl and mix together.

Stir in the bread crumbs, cilantro, and salt and pepper. With your hands, form the mixture into 2-inch by 1-inch cakes and put them on the prepared baking sheet. Bake until the cakes are crisp, about 10 minutes. Serve hot.

PINEAPPLE-GINGER GLAZED SEITAN

*The sweetness of the pineapple and the spiciness of
the ginger have just the right balance to taste great
on seitan, as well as on other plant proteins and
vegetables. Topped with rings of caramelized pineapple,
this beautiful dish is the main event of your Easter
brunch table.*

SERVES 8 TO 10

1 cup pineapple juice
1 cup diced fresh or canned pineapple
⅓ cup ginger juice
1 bunch green onions, white and green parts, chopped
2 tablespoons tamari
2 tablespoons white sesame seeds
2 tablespoons umeboshi plum vinegar
1 clove garlic, chopped
½ teaspoon toasted sesame oil
3 pounds seitan
3 tablespoons grapeseed oil
1 tablespoon extra-virgin olive oil
1 (14-ounce) can pineapple rings, juice reserved
Freshly ground pink peppercorns (optional)

Mix together the pineapple juice, diced pineapple, ginger juice, green onions, tamari, sesame seeds, umeboshi vinegar, garlic, and sesame oil in a large bowl. Pour the mixture over the seitan, coating it evenly. Cover and refrigerate the seitan for at least 4 hours, or overnight.

Heat the grapeseed oil in a large nonstick pan over medium-high heat. When the oil is hot, add the seitan, shaking off any excess marinade, and pan-sear on each side for 2 to 3 minutes. Add the marinade to the pan and cook until the sauce is reduced and the seitan is fully glazed, 5 to 10 minutes.

Heat the olive oil over medium heat in a large sauté pan. Add the pineapple rings and a bit of their juice and cook until lightly browned on the bottom, about 3 minutes. Add a bit more of the reserved juice to the pan, turn the pineapple rings over, and cook for 3 to 4 minutes, until the other side is lightly browned.

Garnish the top of the seitan with pineapple rings, sprinkle with pink peppercorns, and serve.

PASTORAL VANILLA CUPCAKES

*Since vegans don't dye Easter eggs, decorating these
beautiful little white cupcakes is our substitute. The kids
at your party won't miss the eggs, since most kids prefer
cupcakes anyway. We love to decorate them with the
pastel colors of spring using vegan colored sprinkles
and natural food dyes (see photo, page 75). It's fun to
make your own dyes with different vegetable and
fruit juices.*

MAKES 8 CUPCAKES

2 cups unbleached all-purpose flour
2 teaspoons baking powder
½ teaspoon baking soda
¼ teaspoon sea salt
½ cup unrefined sugar
1 cup sunflower oil
2 cups plain unsweetened soy milk
1 tablespoon apple cider vinegar
1 tablespoon vanilla extract

VANILLA–CREAM CHEESE FROSTING
2 cups confectioners' sugar
1 cup Earth Balance Natural Buttery Spread, softened
½ cup baby Thai coconut meat or creamed coconut
1 teaspoon vanilla extract 1 cup vegan cream cheese

Assorted sprinkles, sugars, jimmies, chocolate chips,
  and toasted coconut, for decorating

Preheat the oven to 350°F. Oil 8 cups of a standard
cupcake tin.

Combine the flour, baking powder, baking soda, and salt
in a large bowl.

Combine the sugar, sunflower oil, soy milk, and vinegar in
a blender. Blend until smooth, about 2 minutes. Add to
the dry ingredients and stir gently, being careful not to
overmix. Stir in the vanilla.

Fill the prepared cupcake cups about three-quarters full
with the batter. Bake for 15 minutes, until the cakes are
golden brown and a cake tester comes out clean. Let cool
in the tins.

To make the frosting, mix together the confectioners'
sugar and buttery spread in a large bowl. Set aside.

Combine the coconut meat and vanilla extract in a
blender and blend for 2 minutes. Transfer to a stand
mixer or to a bowl and use a hand mixer. Add the
confectioners' sugar mixture and cream cheese and
mix thoroughly until a smooth frosting is formed.

Remove the cakes from the tins, frost, and decorate
with desired toppings.

STRAWBERRY RHUBARB TARTS with VANILLA BEAN–COCONUT ICE CREAM

The sweet and tart flavors of strawberries and rhubarb are a fantastic combination, and we make fillings and sauces with them all spring and summer long. We especially like to use this filling for pies and tarts. A plate of these mini tarts makes a beautiful presentation and a luscious dessert.

SERVES 8

VANILLA BEAN–COCONUT ICE CREAM

1 cup plain unsweetened soy milk

1 cup soy creamer

1 cup coconut milk

½ cup safflower oil

1 whole vanilla bean

FILLING

5 cups strawberries, hulled and quartered

2 cups diced rhubarb

¾ cup unrefined sugar

1½ tablespoons arrowroot powder

1½ teaspoons ground cinnamon

CRUST

3 cups unbleached all-purpose flour

1 cup Earth Balance Natural Buttery Spread, softened

¼ cup unrefined sugar

2 teaspoons ground cinnamon

2 cups water

To make the ice cream, combine the soy milk, soy creamer, coconut milk, safflower oil, and vanilla bean in a blender and blend for 1 minute. Strain through a sieve into a bowl, put the mixture in the refrigerator, and let it sit until it becomes cold, about 1 hour.

Transfer the mixture to an ice cream maker and freeze according to manufacturer's directions. Remove and store in a bowl in the freezer for at least an hour and up to a week.

Preheat the oven to 350°F.

To make the tart filling, combine the strawberries, rhubarb, sugar, arrowroot, and cinnamon in a large bowl and stir until all well combined.

To make the crust, combine the flour, buttery spread, sugar, cinnamon, and water in a large bowl and stir until well combined and not sticky. Form the dough into a disk.

Roll out the dough on a floured surface to a large circle about ⅛ inch thick. Cut out 8 circles to fit into 4-inch tart pans. Press the dough into the pans and trim any excess dough from the sides. Spoon the filling into the tarts.

Bake for 35 to 40 minutes, until the crust is golden brown. Remove and let cool.

To serve, add a dollop of ice cream to the tarts.

Strawberry Rhubarb Tarts with Vanilla Bean-Coconut Ice Cream (top) and Pastoral Vanilla Cupcakes (bottom, page 73)

CINCO DE MAYO

FIESTA

———

The 5th of May is the day to honor Mexican heritage and pride, and what better way to celebrate than to throw a party and cook up delicious dishes, like crispy tacos, tortilla casserole, tempeh fajitas, and refreshing cocktails and sangria? This is a feast filled with spicy yet subtle flavors that will make you sing and dance the night away.

LA POBLANA SANGRIA

The beautiful city of Puebla, Mexico, is known for its big Cinco de Mayo celebration, and we named our rich and fruity sangria La Poblana in honor of it. Our version is full of beautiful spring berries, tequila, and rosé wine. If you can't find VeeV, an açai berry–based distilled spirit, just substitute an extra 2 ounces of orange liqueur.

SERVES 6

½ cup raspberries
½ cup hulled and sliced strawberries
½ cup blueberries
1 (750 ml) bottle Spanish or Italian rosé wine
3 ounces (6 tablespoons) orange liqueur
3 ounces (6 tablespoons) VeeV açai spirit
2 ounces (¼ cup) tequila silver
5 ounces (10 tablespoons) fresh or bottled peach juice
Ice

Combine the raspberries, strawberries, and blueberries in a carafe or pitcher. Add the wine, orange liqueur, açai spirit, tequila, and peach juice, stir well, and cover. Let the sangria sit for up to 2 days in the refrigerator.

Stir again before serving. Pour the sangria into six rocks glasses filled with ice, spoon in some additional fruit from the carafe, and serve.

LIME TEQUILA SHOOTERS

These small shots are very smooth and refreshing, and serving a round of them is a good way to get your Cinco de Mayo celebration started. They are also cool and refreshing palate cleansers to sip between courses.

SERVES 6

Kosher salt
2 lime wedges
4 ounces silver tequila
2 scoops lime sorbet
4 basil leaves
Ice
6 lime slices, to garnish

Pour the salt onto a small, shallow plate. Rub the outside rims of the shot glasses with the lime wedges. Dip the glasses into the salt to coat the rims.

Combine the tequila, sorbet, and basil in a cocktail shaker. Add ice, shake well, and strain into the prepared glasses. Garnish with the lime slices and serve.

BENITO'S PASSION

Named after Benito Juarez, Mexico's former president and national hero whose leadership made this holiday possible, the blend of fresh juices, mint, and tequila in this cocktail is very cooling and has a nectarlike quality. To release more flavor from the mint leaves, put them in your palm and clap on top of them once.

SERVES 1

1½ ounces añejo tequila
½ ounce agave nectar
¾ ounce passion fruit nectar
1 ounce fresh grapefruit juice
1 ounce fresh orange juice
Ice
3 mint leaves
1 orange peel twist, to garnish

Combine the tequila, agave nectar, passion fruit nectar, grapefruit juice, and orange juice in a cocktail shaker. Add ice and the mint leaves and shake well. Pour into a highball glass without straining. Garnish with the orange peel and serve.

ALBONDIGAS

Albondigas is a Mexican soup that is traditionally made with meatballs and tomato broth, and it's considered a classic comfort food. Here we make wheat balls with ground seitan and peppers and a light roasted tomato and vegetable broth. It makes a beautiful starter for our Cinco de Mayo celebration.

SERVES 8 TO 10

1 pound plum tomatoes, or 1 (14-ounce) can fire-roasted
   tomatoes with juice
2 tablespoons extra-virgin olive oil
1 cup diced yellow onion
1 cup steamed corn kernels
1 bay leaf
1½ teaspoons smoked paprika
1 teaspoon sea salt
4 cups vegetable broth or water
2 tablespoons chopped fresh cilantro, to garnish

WHEAT BALLS

2 tablespoons extra-virgin olive oil, plus more to brush
1 white onion, diced
1 red bell pepper, seeded and diced
1 poblano pepper, seeded and diced
1 pound seitan, drained and cut into 1-inch chunks
⅓ cup unbleached all-purpose flour
⅓ cup dried bread crumbs
1 tablespoon chopped fresh cilantro, plus additional
   to garnish
1 tablespoon sea salt

Preheat the oven to 350°F.

If you are using fresh tomatoes, put them in a roasting pan and roast until softened, about 30 minutes. Remove and let cool.

Peel the tomatoes, transfer to a blender, and blend until smooth.

Heat the olive oil in a large pot over medium heat. Add the onion and corn and sauté for 5 minutes. Add the tomatoes, bay leaf, paprika, and salt. Add the broth and simmer until reduced a bit, 20 to 30 minutes. Remove the bay leaf. The soup can be made ahead of time up to this point. Reheat the soup before serving.

To make the wheat balls, preheat the oven to 300°F. Oil a rimmed baking sheet.

Heat the olive oil in a sauté pan over medium heat. Add the onion, bell pepper, and poblano pepper and sauté until softened, about 5 minutes. Set aside to cool.

Put the seitan in a food processor and process until completely ground. Transfer to a large bowl and stir in the flour, bread crumbs, cilantro, and salt. Add the onion and pepper mixture and stir to combine.

Roll the mixture into 1-inch balls and put them on the prepared baking sheet. Brush the balls with olive oil and put 3 tablespoons of water on the baking sheet.

Bake for 20 to 30 minutes, until lightly browned, and then remove from the oven.

To serve, arrange two wheat balls in each soup bowl and pour the warm tomato soup over them. Garnish with cilantro and serve.

STUFFED AVOCADO SALAD with CHIPOTLE VINAIGRETTE

This refreshing salad is fun to make, and it's a good recipe to experiment with using less familiar vegetables, such as edamame and jicama. The vinaigrette is delicious and full of authentic smoky flavor—we use it to drizzle over dishes like grilled vegetables and rice and beans, too.

SERVES 8

CHIPOTLE VINAIGRETTE

1 cup plus 1 teaspoon extra-virgin olive oil or grapeseed oil
2 shallots, sliced
2 tablespoons fresh lime juice
¼ cup water
1 clove garlic, sliced
1 tablespoon apple cider vinegar
1 teaspoon chipotle chile powder
1 teaspoon smoked paprika
½ teaspoon sea salt
½ teaspoon chopped fresh cilantro
¼ teaspoon chopped fresh oregano

1 large heirloom tomato, diced, or 1 cup cherry tomato halves
1 cup cooked fresh or frozen corn, thawed if frozen
1 cup cooked fresh or frozen peas, thawed if frozen
1 cup chopped cucumber
½ red onion, thinly sliced
1 pound fresh watercress, stemmed
4 ripe avocados, halved, pitted, and peeled
½ cup hemp seeds, to garnish

To make the vinaigrette, heat 1 teaspoon of the olive oil in a sauté pan over medium-high heat, add the shallots, and sauté until soft, about 5 minutes.

Combine the shallots, the remaining 1 cup of oil, the lime juice, water, garlic, vinegar, chipotle powder, smoked paprika, and salt in a blender. Blend until smooth. Transfer to a bowl and stir in the cilantro and oregano.

To prepare the salad, combine the tomato, corn, peas, cucumber, and red onion in a large bowl. Add enough vinaigrette to lightly coat the vegetables and gently toss together.

Arrange the watercress on salad plates and top with the avocado halves. Scoop the vegetable mixture into the center of the avocados. Sprinkle each serving with hemp seeds and drizzle with more vinaigrette to taste.

SPANISH RICE and BLACK BEANS

Rice and beans has been a culinary staple of Latin American countries for centuries, and with good reason. This dish is hearty, healthy, inexpensive, and delicious. Our secret to perfect rice is to slowly simmer the rice with double the amount of liquid.

SERVES 8 TO 10

BEANS

2 cups black beans, rinsed, picked over, and soaked overnight

8 cups water

2 tablespoons sea salt

½ cup finely chopped yellow onion

2 cloves garlic, minced

2 tablespoons safflower oil

Pinch of ground cumin

RICE

3 plum tomatoes, finely chopped

¼ cup diced yellow onion

1 clove garlic, minced

¼ teaspoon dried oregano

2 to 3 cups vegetable broth

3 tablespoons sunflower oil

1½ cups white basmati rice

Sea salt

2 tablespoons chopped fresh cilantro, to garnish

To prepare the beans, drain the beans and transfer to a large pot. Add the water, salt, onion, garlic, oil, and cumin and bring to a boil. Decrease the heat, cover, and simmer until the beans are tender, about 1½ hours.

Combine the tomatoes, onion, garlic, oregano, and 2 cups of the broth in a blender and blend until smooth. Make sure that there is a total of 3 cups of the tomato-broth mixture, adding more broth if necessary. Set aside.

Heat the oil in a saucepan over medium heat. Add the rice and sauté, stirring constantly, until it is lightly browned, about 3 minutes. Make sure that the rice is cooked evenly to keep it from sticking.

Add the tomato mixture and salt to taste to the rice. Stir and bring to a boil. Decrease the heat, cover, and simmer until the rice is tender, about 15 minutes.

Drain the beans of half their cooking liquid. Combine the beans and hot rice in a bowl and toss to combine. Garnish with the cilantro and serve.

CRISPY BLACK BEAN TACOS

It's hard to believe that a snack that tastes this rich and delicious is also very nutritious and low in fat and calories. Serve these tacos with an array of beautiful toppings—we favor avocados, tomatoes, green onions, and radishes, but you can also try chopped cabbage, sautéed greens, pico de gallo, and salsa, to name a few.

SERVES 8 TO 10

2 cups black beans, rinsed, picked over,
  and soaked overnight
8 cups water
1 tablespoon sea salt
¼ cup grapeseed oil
½ cup chopped yellow onion
12 (6-inch) corn tortillas

TOPPINGS

2 avocados, halved, pitted, peeled, and sliced
2 cups chopped tomatoes
1 cup tofu sour cream
½ cup chopped green onions, white and green parts
½ cup sliced radishes
2 jalapeño peppers, seeded and sliced
½ cup chopped fresh cilantro leaves

Drain the beans, rinse, and transfer to a large pot. Add the water and salt. Bring to a boil, decrease the heat, and simmer, covered, until the beans are soft, about 1½ hours. Drain and set aside.

Heat 2 tablespoons of the oil in a large nonstick skillet over medium heat. Add the onion and cook, stirring frequently, until golden brown, about 7 minutes. Add the beans and, with a masher, mash the beans while they are cooking, until they become a rough puree, about 10 minutes. Set aside.

Put the tortillas on a plate and brush both sides of each of them with the remaining 2 tablespoons of the oil. Heat a skillet over medium heat and fry the tortillas, flipping once, until both sides are crisp, but still fairly soft, 1 or 2 minutes per side. Fold the tortillas into taco shapes and set aside.

To serve, fill the tacos with the black bean mixture and serve with the avocados, tomatoes, tofu sour cream, green onions, radishes, jalapeño peppers, and cilantro.

TEMPEH FAJITAS

Here's a quick and easy recipe for tasty fajitas that will make your taste buds dance. For a delicious supper, we like to serve these with Spanish Rice and Black Beans (page 85). Fajitas make great party food because you plate them individually, or let guests roll up their own and add their favorite condiments to customize and add the level of spice they want to bring to the party. Note that when you prepare the tempeh, it needs to parboil in water and tamari before marinating.

SERVES 8 TO 10

MARINADE

½ cup fresh lemon juice

2 cloves garlic, minced

2 tablespoons agave nectar

2 tablespoons tamari

2 cups water

½ cup finely chopped fresh cilantro

¼ cup finely chopped fresh flat-leaf parsley

¼ teaspoon sea salt

4 (8-ounce) packages tempeh, sliced into ¼-inch strips

2 tablespoons tamari

1 tablespoon peeled and chopped fresh ginger

1 tablespoon grapeseed oil

3 bay leaves

6 cilantro sprigs

1 large white onion, sliced in thin strips

1 clove garlic, minced

1 red bell pepper, seeded and cut into thin strips

1 green bell pepper, seeded and cut into thin strips

½ teaspoon chili powder

¼ teaspoon ground cumin

Sea salt and freshly ground black pepper

2 tablespoons extra-virgin olive oil

3 plum tomatoes, peeled, seeded, and diced

1 teaspoon red pepper flakes

¼ cup minced fresh cilantro

20 (6-inch) corn tortillas

Guacamole, pico de gallo, tofu sour cream, and chopped green onions, to garnish

To make the marinade, whisk together the lemon juice, garlic, agave nectar, tamari, water, cilantro, parsley, and salt in a large bowl until combined.

To prepare the tempeh, combine 8 cups of water in a pot with the tempeh, tamari, ginger, grapeseed oil, bay leaves, and cilantro; simmer over medium-low heat for 15 minutes. Drain and discard the bay leaf and cilantro.

Add the tempeh, onion, garlic, red bell pepper, and green bell pepper to the marinade and toss. Add the chili powder, cumin, and salt and pepper to taste and toss again. Let the mixture marinate for 40 minutes.

Heat the olive oil in a large skillet over medium heat. Add the tempeh mixture and cook, stirring, until the vegetables are softened, about 5 minutes. Add the tomatoes and red pepper flakes and cook, stirring, until the tomatoes are softened, about 1 minute. Remove from heat, toss in the cilantro, and place in a bowl for serving.

To warm the tortillas, heat them in a dry skillet over medium heat for 30 seconds on each side. Spoon equal amounts of the tempeh mixture into the center of each tortilla, fold both sides over the filling and roll to close. Garnish the fajitas with guacamole, pico de gallo, tofu sour cream, and chopped green onions and serve.

TORTILLA CASSEROLE

We serve this dish as part of our Cinco de Mayo buffet or for a cozy dinner party. The tangy green sauce made with roasted tomatillos adds an extra dimension of flavor to all of the other layers of goodness. The casserole freezes beautifully and is great to have on hand for an impromptu supper with friends.

SERVES 8 TO 10

1 cup pinto beans, rinsed, picked over, and soaked overnight
4 cups water
1 tablespoon plus 1 teaspoon sea salt
2 pounds tomatillos, husked and rinsed
3 tablespoons extra-virgin olive oil
1 jalapeño pepper, seeded and chopped
½ bunch fresh cilantro, coarsely chopped
2 tablespoons chopped yellow onion
12 (6-inch) corn tortillas
2 zucchinis, thinly sliced
1 pound Mexican-style seitan sausage, chopped
2 cups shredded mozzarella-cheddar vegan cheese blend

Drain the beans, rinse, and transfer to a large pot. Add the water and 1 tablespoon of the salt and bring to a boil. Decrease the heat and cook, partially covered, until the beans are soft, 30 to 40 minutes. Remove from the heat and let cool. Drain and set aside.

Preheat the oven to 350°F. Oil a 7 by 11-inch baking dish.

Put the tomatillos in the baking dish and drizzle with 2 tablespoons of the olive oil. Roast for 30 to 35 minutes, until softened. Remove from the oven and let cool.

Combine the tomatillos, jalapeño pepper, cilantro, and the remaining 1 teaspoon of salt in a blender and blend until smooth.

Heat the remaining 1 tablespoon of the oil in a large sauté pan over medium heat. Add the onion and cook until soft, about 5 minutes. Add the beans, and with a masher or fork, mash them into a puree and stir while they are cooking for about 5 minutes.

To assemble the casserole, spoon some of the tomatillo sauce into the baking dish and cover with 4 tortillas. Top with half of the zucchini slices and spread half of the bean mixture over them. Spread half of the sausage over the beans, spread more sauce over the sausage, and sprinkle with one-third of the cheese. Repeat the layering with the remaining ingredients, ending with a layer of tortillas topped with the remaining sauce and cheese.

Cover with foil and bake for 35 minutes. Uncover and bake for an additional 5 to 10 minutes, until the cheese is lightly browned and bubbly. Remove from the oven and let cool for 10 minutes before serving.

CARAMEL FLAN

Our rendition of the classic Spanish dessert is dairy-free. The rich and creamy custard is made with soy and coconut milk, and the caramel is sweetened with both brown rice syrup and maple syrup. This is a lovely, melt-in-your-mouth treat that you will want to make again and again.

SERVES 10

CARAMEL

2 cups plain unsweetened soy milk

2 (13.5-ounce) cans coconut milk

3 cups brown rice syrup

1½ cups maple syrup

Pinch of sea salt

CUSTARD

2 cups plain unsweetened soy milk

2 (13.5-ounce cans) coconut milk

2 teaspoons agar powder

⅓ cup unrefined sugar

To make the caramel, combine the soy milk, coconut milk, brown rice syrup, maple syrup, and salt in a pot and stir. Bring to a boil and whisk constantly until the mixture thickens, 10 to 20 minutes. Remove and refrigerate for at least 1 hour and up to 3 days.

To make the custard, combine the soy milk, coconut milk, agar, and sugar in a saucepan and mix together. Cook over medium-high heat, stirring occasionally, until just boiling. Remove from the heat and set aside.

Spoon about 1 tablespoon of the caramel each into ten 4-ounce ceramic ramekins and swirl to coat the bottom of each one. Pour the custard into the ramekins and spoon the remaining caramel sauce across the top of each flan. Refrigerate until the flans are firm, at least 1 hour and up to 3 days. To serve, let the ramekins sit out for 20 minutes to come to room temperature.

CINNAMON CHILE CHOCOLATE–DIPPED FRUIT

Fresh fruits dipped in chocolate are a sublime treat. We make them with dairy-free chocolate chips that are available at health food stores and at Whole Foods. Make sure that the fruit is very well dried after rinsing. This will ensure that the chocolate adheres well. We also like to add toasted coconut, cacao nibs, and finely chopped nuts to the freshly dipped fruits before the chocolate sets, for extra delicious taste.

SERVES 8 TO 10

2 cups vegan semisweet chocolate chips

¼ teaspoon ground cinnamon

1 teaspoon ancho chile powder

2 pounds fresh fruit, such as strawberries, kiwifruit, pineapple triangles, and bananas, dried and cut into bite-size pieces

Toasted coconut, cacao nibs, and finely chopped nuts, to garnish (optional)

Line a baking sheet with parchment paper.

Melt the chocolate chips in a double boiler over simmering water, stirring occasionally, until smooth, 3 to 5 minutes. Add the cinnamon and chile powder and stir for 1 more minute. Remove from the heat.

Holding the fruit with a toothpick, dip and twist it in the melted chocolate until one-half to two-thirds is covered. Roll the fruit in one of the toppings and transfer to the prepared baking sheet. Repeat with the rest of the fruit.

Chill the fruit until the chocolate sets, at least 15 minutes, and serve.

4TH OF JULY

BACKYARD BARBECUE

———

Celebrate Independence Day or any other summer day with a vegan-style backyard barbecue. It's the time to hit the farmers' market and serve the cream of the summer's crops—fresh corn, ripe tomatoes, luscious peaches, and berries—the foods that are the best of the season and full of the flavors that we remember all year. We start the party with cooling cocktails and bruschetta, then serve juicy grilled seitan burgers along with chile-crusted corn, crunchy cole slaw, and maple-flavored baked beans. Shortcake with ripe, freshly picked berries is the perfect ending to the meal. This is the essence of summer abundance, so savor the season and let the flavors shine.

RED, WHITE, AND BLUE MARGARITA

This red, white, and blue layered variation on a margarita will get everyone fired up at your next 4th of July barbecue. Soursop, also known as guanabana, is a white-fleshed fruit from South America that lends great color and delicious tropical flavor to the "white" layer of this cocktail. It is available in the frozen foods section of supermarkets and in Latin markets. However, if you can't find it, it can be omitted.

SERVES 1

1½ ounces silver tequila
½ ounce orange liqueur
½ ounce fresh lime juice
½ ounce soursop puree (optional)
Ice
1 ounce cranberry juice
3 blueberries, to garnish

Combine the tequila, orange liqueur, lime juice, and soursop puree in a cocktail shaker. Add ice, shake well, and pour into a rocks glass. Pour the cranberry juice down the side of the glass so that it sinks to the bottom, creating a layered effect. Garnish with blueberries and serve.

PORCH SWING

This refreshing twist on the traditional gin and tonic is a great cocktail for celebrating Independence Day and to welcome summer. We use Greenhook Gin from Greenpoint, Brooklyn, and Q Tonic for this drink because they both have a clean flavor and are not overly sweet. If you can't find VeeV, an açai berry–based distilled spirit, just add an extra half ounce of gin.

SERVES 1

1 mango slice
4 raspberries
4 thyme sprigs
1 ounce gin
1 ounce VeeV açai spirit
Ice
Tonic water
1 mango cube or mango slice, to garnish

Combine the mango slice, raspberries, and 3 of the thyme sprigs in a mixing glass and muddle together. Add the gin, açai spirit, and ice, cover, and shake very well, at least 10 seconds. Pour into a highball glass and top with tonic water. Garnish with mango and the remaining thyme sprig and serve.

1776

This cocktail, made with American whiskey, is a perfect one to celebrate our nation's birthday. Even though whiskey is often considered a cold-weather spirit, when it's mixed with fresh watermelon and lime juices, it is very refreshing on a hot summer day and makes for very easy drinking.

SERVES 1

2 ounces American whiskey, such as Koval
1 ounce fresh lime juice
1 ounce agave nectar
2 ounces fresh watermelon juice
4 cilantro sprigs
Ice

Combine the whiskey, lime juice, agave, watermelon juice, and 3 sprigs of the cilantro in a cocktail shaker. Add ice, shake well, and strain into a rocks glass filled with ice. Garnish with the remaining cilantro sprig and serve.

BRUSCHETTA with WHITE BEAN SPREAD, TOMATOES, and OLIVES

When we make our basic bruschetta, we top it with a mixture of tomatoes, onions, garlic, and olives. What makes it special is the elegant white bean spread made with cannellini beans and a whole head of roasted garlic. It's a great way to greet friends as they arrive at the party. These savory toasts will disappear quickly from the table.

SERVES 8 TO 10; MAKES ABOUT 20 TOASTS

WHITE BEAN SPREAD
1 whole head garlic
½ cup plus 1 tablespoon extra-virgin olive oil
½ cup cannellini beans, rinsed, picked over, and
   soaked overnight
2 cups water
1 bay leaf
¼ teaspoon sea salt
2 teaspoons fresh lemon juice

6 plum tomatoes (about 1 pound), seeded and finely
   chopped
¼ cup chopped red onion
3 cloves garlic, 2 finely minced and 1 peeled
⅓ cup kalamata olives, pitted and chopped
1 tablespoon extra-virgin olive oil
1 teaspoon balsamic vinegar
Sea salt and freshly ground black pepper

1 large baguette
¼ cup extra-virgin olive oil, for brushing
½ cup chopped fresh basil leaves, plus basil leaves
   to garnish

Preheat the oven to 450°F.

To make the white bean spread, cut off the top third of the garlic and rub 1 tablespoon of the olive oil over the garlic. Wrap in aluminum foil and bake for about 45 minutes, until the garlic is very soft. When cool enough to handle, remove the garlic cloves and set aside.

Meanwhile, drain the beans and combine in a large pot with the water, bay leaf, and salt. Bring to a boil, decrease the heat, and simmer, partially covered, until the beans are tender, about 40 minutes. Drain the beans and discard the bay leaf.

Combine the garlic, beans, lemon juice, the remaining ½ cup of olive oil, and salt to taste in a food processor and blend until smooth. Taste and adjust the seasonings, if necessary. The spread can be made ahead of time and stored, covered, in the refrigerator for up to 3 days. Bring to room temperature before serving.

Combine the tomatoes, onion, minced garlic, and olives in a large bowl and toss gently. Add the olive oil, vinegar, and basil and toss again. Add salt and pepper to taste and set aside.

Preheat the oven to 350°F with a rack in the top third of the oven.

Cut the baguette into ½-inch slices on the diagonal and arrange them on a baking sheet. Bake for 3 minutes, turn, and bake for 3 to 4 minutes, until golden brown.

Remove the toasts from the oven and rub the remaining peeled garlic clove on one side of each toast. Brush the toasts with olive oil and top with white bean spread and a spoonful of the tomato mixture. Garnish with fresh basil and serve.

GREEN TOMATO GAZPACHO SHOOTERS

Shooters filled with chilled green tomato gazpacho are a fun and attractive way to start the party. This soup has a nice cool flavor and a bit of a kick that is perfect for waking up your taste buds. We like to use a mix of green field tomatoes and green heirlooms.

MAKES ABOUT 40 (1-OUNCE) SHOOTERS;
OR 8 (1-CUP) SERVINGS

1 pound ripe green tomatoes, coarsely chopped
1 pound green heirloom tomatoes, coarsely chopped
2 cups pineapple juice
1 teaspoon sea salt
½ cup diced red onion
½ cup seeded and diced red bell pepper
½ cup finely diced cucumber
2 tablespoons diced jalapeño pepper
1 clove garlic, coarsely chopped
1 teaspoon sherry vinegar
10 basil leaves, finely chopped
2 tablespoons finely chopped fresh cilantro

AVOCADO-CILANTRO SALAD
1 ripe avocado, halved, pitted, peeled, and diced
1 tablespoon fresh lime juice
2 tablespoons chopped fresh cilantro
Sea salt

Combine the tomatoes, pineapple juice, and salt in a blender and blend until smooth. This may have to be done in batches. Transfer to a large bowl.

Add the onion, bell pepper, cucumber, jalapeño pepper, and garlic to the tomato mixture and stir well. Add the vinegar, basil, and cilantro and stir again. Taste and adjust the seasonings, if necessary. Cover and chill in the refrigerator for at least 8 hours, or overnight.

To make the avocado salad, in a small bowl, mix together the avocado, lime juice, and cilantro with a fork until very smooth. Add salt to taste.

Serve the gazpacho in shooter glasses garnished with a small dollop of the avocado salad.

HERBED HEIRLOOM TOMATO SALAD

We love to make this simple summer salad as soon as we spot heirloom tomatoes at the farmers' markets. When we make it, we mix together as many shades of red, yellow, and green as we can.

SERVES 8 TO 10

2 pounds ripe heirloom tomatoes, cut into
  ½-inch-thick slices
¼ cup extra-virgin olive oil
Juice of ½ lemon
2 tablespoons chopped fresh flat-leaf parsley
2 tablespoons chopped fresh chives
2 tablespoons chopped fresh basil
1 tablespoon finely grated lemon zest
½ teaspoon sea salt
½ teaspoon freshly ground black pepper
1 pound mixed greens or arugula

Put the tomatoes in a nonreactive, shallow dish or bowl. Whisk together the olive oil, lemon juice, parsley, chives, basil, lemon zest, salt, and pepper. Pour the dressing over the tomatoes and gently toss. Let the tomatoes marinate at room temperature for up to 1 hour.

Arrange the greens on individual plates or on a platter. Top with the tomatoes, drizzle with the tomato marinade, and serve.

CREAMY CRUNCHY COLE SLAW

What's a barbecue without a big beautiful bowl of creamy cole slaw? This is our go-to summer salad that complements all kinds of burgers, sandwiches, and sliders. It's best to make the slaw a day ahead of time to let the flavors blend. If you prefer a creamier cole slaw, stir in a bit more vegan mayonnaise before serving.

SERVES 8 TO 12

1 head green cabbage, shredded
2 carrots, peeled and finely shredded
3 large green onions, white and green parts, minced
¾ cup vegan mayonnaise, plus more if needed
1 tablespoon brown mustard
1½ tablespoons red wine vinegar
1 tablespoon agave nectar
1 tablespoon fresh lemon juice
Sea salt and freshly ground black pepper
½ cup chopped fresh flat-leaf parsley
½ cup chopped fresh cilantro
¼ cup toasted white sesame seeds, to garnish

Combine the cabbage, carrots, and green onions in a large bowl and toss together.

Whisk together the mayonnaise, mustard, vinegar, agave, and lemon juice in a bowl until smooth and well blended. Add salt and pepper to taste.

Add the dressing to the cabbage mixture and toss together until combined. Taste and adjust the seasonings, if necessary. Cover and chill in the refrigerator for at least 2 hours, or overnight.

Before serving the slaw, add the parsley and cilantro, and toss well. Taste and adjust the seasonings, if necessary. Add more mayonnaise if it seems dry. Sprinkle the top of the slaw with the sesame seeds and serve. It will keep refrigerated up to 3 days.

BAKED MAPLE PINTO BEANS

We are mad for beans because they are such a great source of protein, there are so many varieties, and they can be prepared in so many different ways. This pinto bean preparation is spiked with the extra smoky flavor of jalapeño and poblano peppers and the sweet goodness of maple syrup. We also like to serve them with vegan hot dogs for a summer franks and beans dinner.

SERVES 8 TO 10

1½ cups dried pinto beans, rinsed, picked over, and soaked overnight in the refrigerator
2 tablespoons extra-virgin olive oil
1 cup finely chopped red onion
1 jalapeño pepper, seeded and diced
1 poblano pepper, seeded and diced
12 cups vegetable stock or water
2 bay leaves
½ cup maple syrup
1 tablespoon blackstrap molasses
1 teaspoon sea salt

Drain and rinse the beans.

Heat the olive oil in a large pot over medium-high heat and add the onion, jalapeño, and poblano. Cook until caramelized, about 10 minutes.

Decrease the heat to medium and add the beans, stock, and bay leaves. Simmer, partially covered, until the beans are tender, about 1½ hours. Remove from the heat and discard the bay leaves. Add the maple syrup, molasses, and salt to the beans and mix together.

Preheat the oven to 350°F.

Transfer the beans and their cooking liquid to a baking dish, cover with aluminum foil, and bake for 45 minutes. Remove the foil and bake until bubbly, 10 to 15 minutes. Serve the beans warm.

CHILE-CRUSTED GRILLED CORN

Corn on the cob is a great summer treat, and we love to grill it and serve it slathered with garlicky chile aïoli, rolled in cashew-almond cheese, and sprinkled with smoky spices. Be sure to have the aïoli, cheese, and spices ready to go as soon as the corn comes off the grill.

SERVES 8 TO 10

CHILE AÏOLI

3 tablespoons plus 2 teaspoons extra-virgin olive oil
4 cloves garlic, minced
2 teaspoons apple cider vinegar
1 cup vegan mayonnaise
½ cup rice milk
2 tablespoons chipotle chile powder
Sea salt and freshly ground black pepper

CASHEW-ALMOND CHEESE

½ cup cashews
½ cup almonds
1 tablespoon fresh lemon juice
1 tablespoon nutritional yeast
Sea salt

2 teaspoons smoked paprika
1 teaspoon chipotle chile powder
16 ears fresh corn, husked
Extra-virgin olive oil, for brushing
Sea salt and freshly ground black pepper

To make the aïoli, heat 2 teaspoons of the olive oil in a small skillet over medium heat. Add the garlic and cook, stirring occasionally, until softened, 3 to 5 minutes. Set aside.

In a medium bowl, whisk together the remaining 3 tablespoons of olive oil and the cider vinegar. Add the garlic, mayonnaise, rice milk, chipotle powder, and salt and pepper to taste; whisk again until smooth. Taste and adjust the seasonings, if necessary. The aïoli can be made a few hours ahead of time. Keep covered in the refrigerator and bring to room temperature before serving.

To make the cheese, preheat the oven to 300°F. Spread out the cashews and almonds on a baking sheet and bake for 15 to 20 minutes, until golden brown. Transfer the nuts to a food processor and pulse until coarsely chopped. Add the lemon juice, nutritional yeast, and salt to taste and pulse again to mix. Spread the mixture in a large flat dish.

In a separate small bowl, mix together the smoked paprika and chipotle powder.

Brush each ear of corn generously with olive oil and season with salt and pepper.

Prepare a gas or charcoal grill or heat a grill pan over medium-high heat. Lay the corn on the grill rack and grill for 6 to 10 minutes, turning several times, until lightly charred and tender.

Brush the grilled ears of corn generously with the aïoli, roll them in the cheese, sprinkle with the spice mixture, and serve at once.

JALAPEÑO RED PEPPER CORNBREAD STICKS

Cornbread infused with the flavors of jalapeño and local red bell peppers is a fantastic starter or side for a summer outdoor party. Serve the sticks warm or lightly toasted and slathered with vegan butter. And if you have any left over, they're great to serve for the next morning's breakfast.

SERVES 8 TO 10

1 cup yellow cornmeal
1 cup unbleached all-purpose flour
⅓ cup unrefined sugar
1 tablespoon baking powder
½ teaspoon sea salt
1 cup plain unsweetened soy milk
¼ cup sunflower oil
1 tablespoon Earth Balance Natural Buttery Spread, melted
3 jalapeño peppers, seeded and diced
1 red bell pepper, seeded and diced

Preheat the oven to 350°F. Oil a 7 by 11-inch baking dish and a large baking sheet.

Combine the cornmeal, flour, sugar, baking powder, and salt in a large bowl and mix together. Add the soy milk, oil, buttery spread, jalapeño peppers, and red bell pepper and mix together. Pour the mixture into the prepared baking dish.

Bake for 30 to 35 minutes, until the top is lightly browned. Remove from the oven and let cool.

Cut the cornbread into 1-inch by 3-inch sticks. Put them on the prepared baking sheet and return them to the oven to bake another 15 to 25 minutes, until the cornbread is golden brown on all of the edges. Serve warm.

BIG BARBECUE SEITAN BURGERS

We love to fire up the grill and make these big juicy seitan burgers dipped in spicy chipotle barbecue sauce. We keep this smoky sauce on hand all summer to serve with grilled vegetables, tofu, and rice and beans. Grab a cold organic beer, pile your burger high with all the fixin's, and dig in!

MAKES 12 BURGERS

BARBECUE SAUCE

1 cup ketchup
1 (7-ounce) can tomato paste
½ cup extra-virgin olive oil
½ cup tamari
½ cup blackstrap molasses
¼ cup agave nectar
1 tablespoon brown rice vinegar
1 tablespoon apple cider vinegar
1½ teaspoons chipotle chile powder
2 tablespoons water

BURGERS

2 pounds seitan
3 tablespoons extra-virgin olive oil
2 cups diced white onion
2 cups diced celery
1 cup unbleached all-purpose flour
¼ cup nutritional yeast
2 teaspoons minced garlic
2 tablespoons chopped fresh flat-leaf parsley
2 tablespoons chopped fresh cilantro
1 teaspoon sea salt

12 burger buns
Roasted Poblano Guacamole (page 7), sliced red onions and tomatoes, caramelized onions, and tempeh bacon, to serve

To make the sauce, combine the ketchup, tomato paste, olive oil, tamari, molasses, agave, brown rice vinegar, cider vinegar, chipotle powder, and water in a blender and blend until smooth. Transfer to a large saucepan and bring to a boil over medium-high heat. Reduce the heat and simmer, stirring occasionally, until the sauce is thickened and reduced, about 20 minutes. The sauce can be made ahead of time, and it will keep, covered, in the refrigerator, for up to 1 week.

To make the burgers, put the seitan in a food processor and blend until finely ground. Set aside in a bowl.

Heat 2 tablespoons of the olive oil in a sauté pan over medium heat. Add the onion and celery and cook until softened, 5 to 10 minutes. Add to the seitan and stir. Add the flour, nutritional yeast, garlic, parsley, cilantro, and salt and mix thoroughly. Form the mixture into 12 (4-inch) patties and refrigerate for 45 minutes.

Heat a gas or charcoal grill or a grill pan over medium heat. If using a grill pan, brush with the remaining 1 tablespoon of olive oil.

Put the sauce in a shallow bowl. Dip the patties in the sauce and grill over medium-high heat for 2 to 4 minutes a side, until the edges darken and crisp and the patties are warmed through.

Serve the burgers with the burger buns and toppings.

MOJO DE AJO SEITAN with GRILLED PEACHES

Mojo de ajo is a pungent garlic marinade or sauce made with roasted and raw garlic, fresh herbs, oil, and vinegar. It's good to have a jar on hand all summer to marinate seitan, tofu, and vegetables for grilling and to drizzle over fresh tomatoes and greens. The marinade will keep, covered, in the refrigerator for up to 3 days. In this dish, the fruitiness of grilled peaches adds a perfect sweet complement to the garlicky seitan.

SERVES 8 TO 10

MOJO DE AJO MARINADE
½ cup plus 3 cloves garlic, peeled
½ cup extra-virgin olive oil
½ cup sunflower oil
½ cup apple cider vinegar
2 tablespoons chopped fresh flat-leaf parsley
2 tablespoons chopped fresh cilantro
½ teaspoon chopped fresh oregano
½ teaspoon chopped fresh thyme
4 bay leaves
1 teaspoon sea salt
1 teaspoon freshly ground black pepper

2 pounds seitan, sliced ½ inch thick
1½ pounds ripe peaches, halved and pitted
3 tablespoons extra-virgin olive oil
1 tablespoon chopped fresh chives
½ teaspoon smoked paprika
½ teaspoon sea salt
½ teaspoon freshly ground black pepper

Preheat the oven to 350°F.

To make the marinade, toss the ½ cup of the garlic cloves with the olive oil in a baking dish and roast for 25 minutes. Let cool.

Combine the roasted garlic and olive oil, the remaining 3 garlic cloves, the sunflower oil, cider vinegar, parsley, cilantro, oregano, thyme, bay leaves, salt, and pepper in a blender and blend until smooth.

Put the seitan slices in a bowl and cover with the marinade. Cover and marinate for at least 2 hours, or overnight in the refrigerator.

Put the peach halves in a mixing bowl. Add the olive oil, chives, paprika, salt, and pepper and toss together. Let the mixture rest for a few minutes.

Prepare a gas or charcoal grill or heat a grill pan over medium-high heat. Grill the peaches until grill marks appear, about 3 minutes per side. Remove and set aside. Grill the seitan until grill marks appear, 2 or 3 minutes per side.

Arrange the seitan on a platter or individual plates, top with the grilled peach halves, and serve.

RED, WHITE, and BLUE SHORTCAKE

Celebrate the stars and stripes with a rich and festive cake. You can serve the cake on a plate or a cake stand, but we like to make it in a glass trifle bowl, layered decoratively with whipped cream and fresh ripe summer berries.

SERVES 10 TO 12

1 cup plain unsweetened soy milk
1 cup sunflower oil
1 cup unrefined sugar
½ teaspoon apple cider vinegar
1 cup unbleached all-purpose flour
1½ teaspoons baking powder
1¼ cups whole strawberries, hulled
1¼ cups blackberries
1 cup blueberries

WHIPPED CREAM
1 cup baby Thai coconut meat or ½ cup creamed coconut
½ cup coconut milk
1 teaspoon vanilla extract
2 cups vegan cream cheese
2 cups confectioners' sugar
1 cup Earth Balance Natural Buttery Spread, melted

Preheat the oven to 350°F. Oil 2 (6-inch) cake pans.

To make the cake, combine the soy milk, oil, sugar, and cider vinegar in a blender and blend for 3 minutes.

Combine the flour and baking powder in a large mixing bowl. Add the wet mixture and mix together until well blended. Do not overmix.

Pour the mixture evenly into the cake pans and bake for 35 minutes, until a cake tester comes out clean. Put the cakes in the refrigerator to cool for 10 minutes before removing from the pans to serve.

Put the berries in a large bowl and toss together.

To make the whipped cream, combine the coconut meat, coconut milk, and vanilla in a blender and blend until smooth. Transfer the mixture to a stand mixer or a large bowl. Add the cream cheese, confectioners' sugar, and buttery spread. Using the stand mixer or a hand mixer, beat together on high speed until peaks form.

To assemble the cake, put one cake in a trifle bowl or on a large round plate. Spread a layer of whipped cream over the top and add a layer of half the berries. Top with the remaining cake and the whipped cream. Decorate the top of the cake with the remaining berries. Chill in the refrigerator for at least 1 hour, or up to 2 days, before serving.

THANKSGIVING

———

Thanksgiving has always been a very special holiday to us and to our Candle family of restaurants. For more than twenty-five years, this day has been one of the busiest and most rewarding, whether our customers dine in with their families, take out our specialties for their celebrations at home, or "veganize" their dinners with recipes from our cookbooks. This is the time for us to join together and show gratitude to the farmers who bring us the bounty of autumn, to savor great plant-based food, and to give heartfelt thanks for our friends and families.

MIDNIGHT CARRIAGE

———

This cocktail is full of fall flavors, including pumpkin, cinnamon, and nutmeg. It's a good one to serve before Thanksgiving dinner or afterward with dessert. Be sure to drink it before midnight—before your chariot turns back into a pumpkin.

SERVES 1

2 ounces bourbon
2 tablespoons pumpkin puree
1 tablespoon coconut milk
¼ ounce maple syrup
½ ounce apple juice
¼ ounce Pedro Ximenez sweet sherry
Pinch of ground cinnamon
Ice
Pinch of freshly grated nutmeg, to garnish

Combine the bourbon, pumpkin puree, coconut milk, maple syrup, apple juice, sherry, and cinnamon in a cocktail shaker. Add ice, shake well, and strain into a chilled martini glass. Garnish with the nutmeg and serve.

HARVEST PUNCH BOWL

———

Serving a festive autumn punch garnished with rum-infused apples and pears is a lovely way to start your Thanksgiving celebration. Our bartenders have created this deep-flavored infused rum, and it is the base for a number of cocktails that we serve during the holiday season. You will definitely want to keep a jar on hand. For the punch, raspberry juice or syrup is a good substitute for framboise.

SERVES 16

APPLE AND PEAR RUM INFUSION
1 apple, cored and thinly sliced
1 pear, cored and thinly sliced
1 (750 ml) bottle spiced rum

12 ounces (1½ cups) orange liqueur
6 ounces (¾ cup) framboise liqueur
1 (750 ml) bottle light-bodied red wine, such as Pinot Noir
18 ounces (2¼ cups) apple juice
1 apple, cored and thinly sliced
1 pear, cored and thinly sliced
Ice

To make the infusion, put the sliced fruit in a clean glass container, add the rum, and cover tightly. Let the infusion sit for 3 days. Strain the rum and reserve the fruit.

To make the punch, pour the infused rum, orange liqueur, framboise, wine, and apple juice into a punch bowl and stir well. Add the sliced apple and pear and let it sit for about 2 hours.

Serve the punch with ice, garnished with the reserved apple and pear slices.

ROASTED SQUASH SOUP with ALMOND CREAM and SPICED PUMPKIN SEEDS

This smooth and creamy soup, garnished with rich almond cream and toasted pumpkin seeds, makes an elegant starter for a Thanksgiving feast. We recommend making batches of this nourishing soup all season long and keeping it on hand (it freezes beautifully) for cozy dinners that will warm your heart and soul. Note that the almonds must be soaked overnight.

SERVES 8 TO 10

ALMOND CREAM
2 cups sliced almonds
3 tablespoons safflower oil
2 tablespoons fresh lemon juice
1½ teaspoons sea salt
½ cup water
1 tablespoon chopped fresh chives

ROASTED SQUASH SOUP
3 tablespoons extra-virgin olive oil
1 tablespoon Earth Balance Natural Buttery Spread
1 cup diced white onion
1 cup chopped apple
¼ teaspoon ground cinnamon
¼ teaspoon chipotle chile powder
¼ teaspoon chopped fresh sage
¼ teaspoon fresh rosemary
½ lemongrass stalk, split
1½ teaspoons sea salt
3 pounds butternut squash, peeled, seeded, and cut into 1-inch pieces
8 cups vegetable stock

SPICED PUMPKIN SEEDS
1 cup pumpkin seeds, hulled
1 tablespoon extra-virgin olive oil
1½ teaspoons fresh lemon juice
Pinch of ground cinnamon
Sea salt and freshly ground black pepper

To make the cream, the day before serving, put the almonds in a bowl and add enough water to cover them. Cover and let soak overnight in the refrigerator.

Drain the nuts and transfer to a blender. Add the oil, lemon juice, salt, and water and blend until smooth, about 5 minutes. Transfer to a bowl, stir in the chives, and set aside. The cream will keep, covered, in the refrigerator for up to 2 days.

To make the soup, heat the oil and buttery spread in a large soup pot over medium heat. Add the onion, apple, cinnamon, chipotle powder, sage, rosemary, lemongrass, and salt and cook, stirring occasionally, for 5 minutes.

Add the squash to the pot and stir to coat, about 3 minutes. Add the stock, bring to a boil, decrease the heat, and simmer, covered, until the squash is tender, about 40 minutes. Remove the lemongrass stalk and let the soup cool.

Transfer the soup to a blender and blend until smooth. Or blend the soup with an immersion blender until smooth. This will have to be done in batches. The soup can be made ahead of time up to this point. It will keep in the refrigerator for up to 3 days or frozen up to 3 months.

Meanwhile, preheat the oven to 300°F.

To prepare the pumpkin seeds, combine the seeds, oil, lemon juice, cinnamon, and salt and pepper to taste in a bowl and mix together. Transfer to a baking sheet and roast for 5 to 10 minutes, shaking the pan occasionally, until the seeds are lightly browned.

To serve, pour the warm soup into bowls. Add a dollop of the almond cream and sprinkle with the roasted pumpkin seeds.

TRICOLOR BEET SALAD with HORSERADISH DRESSING

Nothing beats beets! We use a variety of them, from dark red to golden to striped chioggias, and the beet greens, too, when we make this gorgeous salad. The horseradish dressing adds just the right tangy finish to the sweet beets. The dressing can be made ahead of time and will keep, covered, in the refrigerator for up to 3 days. Bring to room temperature before using.

SERVES 8 TO 10

HORSERADISH DRESSING
1 teaspoon extra-virgin olive oil
½ cup sliced shallots
8 ounces silken tofu
½ cup peeled and finely diced fresh horseradish
½ cup extra-virgin olive oil
⅓ cup white wine vinegar
1 teaspoon sea salt

6 beets, such as red, gold, and chioggia, trimmed,
   greens reserved
1 cup pecans
1 pound green beans, trimmed and cut into 2-inch pieces
2 tablespoons extra-virgin olive oil
1 small fennel bulb, trimmed, cored, and thinly sliced
1 apple, cored and thinly sliced, to serve
1 cup dried cranberries

To make the dressing, heat the olive oil in a sauté pan over medium-high heat and cook the shallots until softened, about 5 minutes. Add the tofu and cook for 2 minutes. Remove from the heat and let cool.

Transfer the shallot-tofu mixture to a blender. Add the horseradish, olive oil, vinegar, and salt and blend until smooth. Add a bit of water to the dressing if it seems too thick.

Preheat the oven to 350°F.

Wrap each beet individually in aluminum foil and roast for about 1 hour, until fork-tender. Let cool. Peel the beets and cut into 1-inch dice.

To toast the pecans, spread them out on a baking sheet and toast them in a preheated 350°F oven or toaster oven for about 5 minutes, until golden brown and fragrant, shaking the pan once or twice for even toasting. Slide the nuts off the baking sheet as soon as they reach the desired color to stop the cooking.

Bring 8 cups of water to a boil in a saucepan over medium-high heat. Add the beans and cook until tender, 5 to 8 minutes. Drain, rinse under cold water, and set aside.

Rinse the reserved beet greens and chop coarsely. Heat the oil in a large sauté pan over medium-high heat. Add the beet greens and cook until wilted and tender, about 2 minutes.

Transfer the beet greens to a large salad bowl. Add the beets, green beans, and fennel and toss together. Add enough dressing to coat the salad and toss again.

To serve, arrange the salad on salad plates. Top each serving with apples, pecans, and cranberries and drizzle with additional dressing.

ROASTED BRUSSELS SPROUT SALAD with APPLES, CRANBERRIES, and MAPLE-CAYENNE DRESSING

The reason that brussels sprouts sometimes get a bad rap is that they are usually overcooked. In our version, the sprouts are gently roasted with olive oil and fresh rosemary so they develop a mild nutty flavor. Then we toss them with a delectable maple dressing, apples, dried cranberries, and toasted almonds. We guarantee that this crunchy holiday salad will convert the most diehard brussels sprout doubters.

SERVES 8 TO 10

3 pounds brussels sprouts, trimmed and halved

¼ cup extra-virgin olive oil

½ teaspoon chopped fresh rosemary

½ teaspoon sea salt

¼ teaspoon freshly ground black pepper

4 shallots, sliced

MAPLE-CAYENNE DRESSING

½ cup grapeseed oil

¼ cup white wine vinegar

3 tablespoons maple syrup

¼ cup water

¼ teaspoon cayenne pepper

¼ teaspoon sea salt

1 teaspoon chopped fresh flat-leaf parsley

1 teaspoon chopped fresh thyme

2 red apples, cored and thinly sliced

1 cup dried cranberries

1 cup chopped roasted almonds

Preheat the oven to 350°F.

Put the brussels sprouts in a large bowl, add the olive oil, rosemary, salt, and pepper and toss together. Transfer to a roasting pan and cover with aluminum foil. Roast for about 20 minutes, until just tender.

Remove from the oven, discard the foil, and sprinkle the shallots over the sprouts. Roast for an additional 15 minutes. Remove and let cool.

To make the dressing, combine the oil, vinegar, maple syrup, water, cayenne pepper, and salt in a blender and blend until smooth. Transfer to a bowl, add the parsley and thyme, and whisk together.

Combine the brussels sprouts, apple slices, cranberries, and almonds in a large bowl. Add the dressing, toss together, and serve.

PUMPKIN SEED–CRUSTED TEMPEH with ROASTED GINGER-MAPLE SWEET POTATOES and CRANBERRY-ORANGE RELISH

This colorful dish takes full advantage of all of the autumnal flavor elements, from sweet potatoes baked with maple syrup and fresh herbs, to earthy tempeh cooked in a pumpkin seed crust, to the sprightly, slightly acidic cranberry relish topping.

SERVES 8 TO 10

CRANBERRY-ORANGE RELISH

3 tablespoons extra-virgin olive oil

2 cups fresh or frozen cranberries, coarsely chopped

1 cup chopped fennel

2 tablespoons maple syrup

1 red apple, cored and chopped

3 oranges, peeled and segmented, juices reserved

1 tablespoon chopped fresh flat-leaf parsley

1 tablespoon chopped fresh chives

Pinch of ground cinnamon

Sea salt and freshly ground black pepper

ROASTED GINGER-MAPLE SWEET POTATOES

6 pounds sweet potatoes, peeled and quartered

2 tablespoons extra-virgin olive oil

2 tablespoons Earth Balance Natural Buttery Spread, melted

1 tablespoon maple syrup

2 tablespoons peeled and chopped fresh ginger

1/2 teaspoon ground cinnamon

4 fresh sage leaves, chopped

1 tablespoon chopped fresh rosemary

1/4 teaspoon sea salt

4 (8-ounce) packages tempeh

4 2/3 cups water

2 tablespoons tamari

1 tablespoon peeled and chopped fresh ginger

1 tablespoon grapeseed oil

3 bay leaves

1 tablespoon fresh cilantro leaves

2 cups pumpkin seeds, hulled

1 cup unbleached all-purpose flour

1/2 teaspoon sea salt

1/4 teaspoon freshly ground black pepper

1/4 cup Ener-G egg replacer

1/2 cup extra-virgin olive oil

To prepare the relish, heat the oil in a large sauté pan over medium heat. Add the cranberries and fennel and cook until the cranberries begin to pop and the fennel is softened, 10 to 15 minutes. Remove from the heat and stir in the maple syrup. Transfer to a bowl and add the apple, oranges and their juice, parsley, chives, cinnamon, and salt and pepper to taste and mix together. The relish can be made up to 3 days ahead and will keep, covered, in the refrigerator.

Preheat the oven to 350°F.

To prepare the sweet potatoes, put them in a large bowl. Add the oil, buttery spread, maple syrup, ginger, cinnamon, sage, rosemary, and salt and toss together to coat the potatoes.   continued

Transfer to a baking dish and cover with aluminum foil. Bake for about 1 hour, until the potatoes are fork-tender.

Meanwhile, to prepare the tempeh, cut each tempeh block in half horizontally, then cut into 3 equal pieces vertically. You will have 6 pieces per block of tempeh.

Combine the tempeh, 4 cups of the water, tamari, ginger, oil, bay leaves, and cilantro in a large pot and simmer over medium-low heat for 15 to 20 minutes. Drain and set aside.

Combine the pumpkin seeds, flour, salt, and pepper in a food processor and process until coarsely ground, 3 to 5 minutes. Transfer to a shallow bowl.

Mix together the egg replacer and the remaining $2/3$ cup of water in a shallow bowl. Dredge the tempeh in the egg replacer mixture, covering both sides. Dip the tempeh into the pumpkin seed crust and pat firmly to cover all sides completely. Let the tempeh sit for 5 minutes to ensure that the crust has adhered to it properly.

Heat the olive oil in a sauté pan over medium-high heat. Add the tempeh and cook until crisp and golden brown, 1 to 2 minutes per side. Transfer the tempeh to a plate lined with paper towels to absorb any excess oil.

To serve, arrange the sweet potatoes and tempeh on plates and garnish with a dollop of cranberry relish.

PORCINI-CRUSTED SEITAN with GLAZED CIPOLLINI ONIONS and MUSHROOM GRAVY

We love to serve these elegant breaded seitan cutlets for the holidays. The seitan marinates in a fragrant blend of lemon and herbs before being breaded and fried. It pairs perfectly with roasted and glazed cipollinis and rich mushroom gravy. We give thanks for this deeply delicious plate of food.

SERVES 8 TO 10

2 pounds seitan, sliced into
½-inch-thick cutlets

2 tablespoons fresh
lemon juice

1 tablespoon chopped garlic

½ teaspoon chopped fresh
rosemary

½ teaspoon sea salt

¼ teaspoon freshly ground
black pepper

2 cups unbleached
all-purpose flour

1 tablespoon porcini
mushroom powder

⅓ cup extra-virgin olive oil,
plus more if needed

MUSHROOM GRAVY

1 tablespoon extra-virgin
olive oil

1 tablespoon Earth Balance
Natural Buttery Spread

3 tablespoons chopped
shallots

3 cups sliced cremini
mushrooms

2 tablespoons unbleached
all-purpose flour

½ cup white wine

2 cups vegetable stock

GLAZED CIPOLLINI ONIONS

2 pounds cipollini onions,
peeled

1 tablespoon extra-virgin
olive oil

6 cloves garlic, chopped

2 tablespoons unrefined
sugar

1 tablespoon maple syrup

1 sprig thyme, chopped

1 sprig rosemary, chopped

Sea salt and freshly ground
black pepper

To prepare the cutlets, put the seitan in a large bowl. Whisk together the lemon juice, garlic, rosemary, salt, and pepper in a small bowl. Pour over the seitan, cover, and marinate in the refrigerator for at least 4 hours, or overnight.

Preheat the oven to 350°F. Oil a rimmed baking sheet.

To make the gravy, heat the olive oil and buttery spread in a large saucepan over medium heat. Add the shallots and mushrooms and cook, stirring occasionally, until the shallots are translucent, 5 to 10 minutes. Add the flour and cook for 2 minutes, stirring constantly, to make a roux. Add the wine and stock to deglaze the pan and cook over medium heat until the sauce thickens, 10 to 15 minutes.

To prepare the onions, combine the onions, oil, garlic, sugar, maple syrup, thyme, rosemary, and salt and pepper to taste in a large bowl and toss together to coat the onions.

Transfer the mixture to the prepared baking sheet. Cover with aluminum foil and roast for 20 minutes. Remove the foil and return the onions to the oven for an additional 15 minutes.

Meanwhile, mix the flour and porcini powder together in a shallow bowl. Dredge the seitan in the flour mixture to coat evenly.

Heat the olive oil in a large sauté pan over medium-high heat. Add a few seitan cutlets and cook for 2 minutes on each side. Remove the seitan and place on paper towels to absorb any excess oil. Repeat with the remaining seitan, adding more oil if necessary.

To serve, arrange the seitan and glazed onions on a plate and spoon the mushroom gravy over them.

WILD RICE and CORNBREAD STUFFING

This sweet and savory side dish is chock full of Thanksgiving staples—cornbread, wild rice, cranberries, and apples. It's best to use stale bread for stuffing because it absorbs flavors and has a better texture, so make the cornbread a day or two in advance. The stuffing can be made a few hours ahead of time and kept warm in the oven until you are ready to serve the feast.

SERVES 8 TO 10

2 cups wild rice, soaked for 2 hours and drained

4 cups water

3 tablespoons extra-virgin olive oil

½ cup finely diced yellow onion

1 cup finely diced carrots

1 cup finely diced celery

2 teaspoons chopped fresh sage

2 teaspoons chopped fresh rosemary

½ cup finely diced apple

1 cup dried cranberries

¼ teaspoon ground cinnamon

1 teaspoon sea salt

¼ teaspoon freshly ground black pepper

3 cups stale cornbread (page 104, omit the jalapeño and red bell peppers), cubed

Combine the rice and water in a large pot, making sure that there is enough water to cover the rice. Bring to a boil over high heat, decrease the heat, and simmer, covered, until the rice is tender, 45 to 60 minutes. Drain and set aside.

Heat the olive oil in a large pot over medium-high heat. Add the onion, carrots, celery, sage, and rosemary and cook, stirring occasionally, for 5 minutes. Add the wild rice, apple, cranberries, cinnamon, salt, and pepper and cook, stirring occasionally, for an additional 10 to 15 minutes. Stir in the cornbread cubes and cook for another 5 minutes. Serve in a large bowl.

PECAN PIE with CINNAMON ICE CREAM

Our pecan pie is a vegan version of the holiday classic. It is sweet, simple, and oozes with pecans glazed with maple syrup instead of sticky corn syrup. This is an irresistible dessert, especially when topped with a scoop of soy- and coconut-based cinnamon ice cream.

SERVES 8 TO 10

CINNAMON ICE CREAM

1 whole vanilla bean
1 cup plain unsweetened soy milk
1 cup soy creamer
½ cup safflower oil
1 cup coconut milk
1 teaspoon ground cinnamon

PIECRUST

1½ cups unbleached all-purpose flour
1½ tablespoons unrefined sugar
6 tablespoons Earth Balance Natural Buttery Spread, melted
1 teaspoon ground cinnamon
¼ teaspoon sea salt
6 tablespoons cold water

FILLING

1 cup plain unsweetened soy milk
1 cup coconut milk
1½ cups brown rice syrup
¾ cup maple syrup
Pinch of sea salt
1 tablespoon arrowroot powder
3 cups whole pecans

To make the ice cream, split the vanilla bean down the center with a small, sharp knife. Scrape out the seeds and put them in a blender. Add the soy milk, soy creamer, safflower oil, coconut milk, and cinnamon and blend for 2 minutes. Strain the mixture through a fine sieve.

Transfer the mixture to an ice cream maker and freeze according to the manufacturer's instructions. Remove and store in a bowl in the freezer for at least an hour and up to a week.

To make the crust, combine the flour, sugar, buttery spread, cinnamon, salt, and water in a large bowl and stir together gently until incorporated. Form the dough into a ball. On a lightly floured surface, roll the dough with a rolling pin into a 12-inch circle about ¼ to ⅛ inch thick. Transfer the dough to an oiled 9-inch pie pan and trim the edges, leaving about an extra inch hanging over the edge. Tuck the overhanging dough underneath itself to form a thick edge that is even with the rim and flute as desired. Put the piecrust in the refrigerator and chill for 1 hour.

To make the filling, combine the soy milk, coconut milk, brown rice syrup, maple syrup, and salt in a saucepan and cook over medium-high heat until boiling. Decrease the heat and let the mixture simmer, stirring occasionally, until it becomes a dark caramel, about 1 hour and 20 minutes. If the caramel doesn't seem thick enough, simmer and reduce it a bit longer. Stir in the arrowroot powder.

Preheat the oven to 350°F.

Put the pecans in a large bowl, pour in 1½ cups of the caramel sauce, and mix together. Spoon the mixture into the piecrust. Bake for 30 to 35 minutes, until the crust and filling are lightly browned. Let stand for 2 hours at room temperature. To serve, cut the pie into wedges and top with the cinnamon ice cream.

PUMPKIN CHEESECAKE with APPLE CIDER REDUCTION

Be sure to save room for this fantastic cheesecake, a creative dessert that uses classic Thanksgiving ingredients—pumpkin, apple cider, cinnamon, and nutmeg. The pie and frosting can be made up to 2 days ahead of time.

SERVES 8 TO 10

4 cups vegan cream cheese
2 cups agave nectar or maple syrup
2 cups plain unsweetened soy milk
1 cup pumpkin puree
1½ cups (12 ounces) silken tofu
1 cup arrowroot powder
1 tablespoon agar powder
1 teaspoon ground cinnamon
½ teaspoon freshly grated nutmeg

APPLE CIDER REDUCTION

4 cups apple cider
1 cup unrefined sugar
¼ teaspoon freshly grated nutmeg

½ recipe Vanilla-Cream Cheese Frosting (page 73), (optional)

Preheat the oven to 350°F. Wrap aluminum foil around the bottom and halfway up the sides of a 9-inch springform pan to prevent any leaking.

Combine the cream cheese, agave, soy milk, pumpkin, tofu, arrowroot, agar, cinnamon, and nutmeg in a large mixing bowl and stir together. Transfer to a blender and blend until smooth and ingredients are fully integrated. This may have to be done in batches. Pour the mixture into the prepared springform pan.

Put the cheesecake in a large baking pan and fill the pan halfway with hot water. Bake for about 2 hours, until lightly browned. Remove, let cool, cover, and refrigerate. The cheesecake can be made up to 2 days ahead of time.

To make the cider reduction, combine the cider, sugar, and nutmeg in a pot and bring to a simmer over medium heat. Simmer, stirring occasionally, until the mixture is reduced by half and is syrupy, 1 to 1½ hours. The reduction can be made and refrigerated up to 2 hours ahead of time. Bring to room temperature before serving.

To serve, remove the foil from the pan. Run a knife around the outer edge of the cheesecake and release the springform pan clamp. Put the cake on a plate or cake stand. Pipe or spread the top of the cheesecake with the frosting. Drizzle the reduction over the cheesecake. Cut into wedges and serve.

CHRISTMAS

The Christmas season is full of high spirits and anticipation
as we gather our loved ones together on Christmas Eve
and Christmas Day to savor the holiday. What better gift to
give to them than wonderful food and drink? Pomegranate
punch and eggnog fill us with warmth and good cheer
as we nibble on savory appetizers before sitting down
to a special dinner. And, of course, there are cups of hot
chocolate to sip and plates of Christmas cookies to eat
while we open presents and bask in the joy of the season.

CHRISTMAS POMEGRANATE PUNCH

We love to make punch for the holidays. It's our chance to pull out the big punch bowl that just takes up space the rest of the year. This festive drink blends rum with pomegranate juice and hibiscus tea and resembles a glühwein (German mulled wine), but it is served chilled.

SERVES 10 TO 12

1 (750 ml) bottle rum
12 ounces (1½ cups) triple sec
32 ounces (4 cups) pomegranate juice
12 ounces (1½ cups) spicy red wine, such as Malbec
  or Shiraz
½ cup hibiscus tea leaves
16 ounces (2 cups) hot water
16 cinnamon sticks
2 teaspoons whole cloves
3 lemons, cut into wedges, to garnish
Ice

Combine the rum, triple sec, pomegranate juice, and wine in a punch bowl and stir.

Steep the hibiscus leaves in the hot water for 5 minutes. Strain the tea into a bowl, pressing the leaves until dry. Pour it into the punch bowl and stir. Put 4 of the cinnamon sticks and ½ teaspoon of the cloves in a piece of cheesecloth and tie tightly. Let it sit in the punch for about an hour, then remove.

Stud the lemon wedges with the remaining cloves. Pour the punch into cups or small glasses over ice. Garnish each serving with the remaining cinnamon sticks and the lemon wedges and serve.

HOLIDAY FLIP

This spiked nog, laced with the fragrant holiday flavors of nutmeg and cinnamon, is our vegan version of traditional eggnog. It's a flip because it can be heated; the original flip was a rum drink heated with an iron, though we recommend using your stove. The heating meant it had been "flipped." This winter warmer is just the thing to drink by the fireside on a cold Christmas night.

SERVES 1

1½ ounces bourbon
2½ ounces soy creamer
2 sage leaves
3 whole cloves
Pinch of freshly grated nutmeg
Pinch of ground cinnamon
Pinch of freshly ground black pepper
Ice
1 cinnamon stick, to garnish

Combine the bourbon, soy creamer, sage leaves, cloves, nutmeg, ground cinnamon, and pepper in a cocktail shaker. Add ice, shake well, and strain into a rocks glass. Garnish with a cinnamon stick and serve.

Variation: To serve this warm, simmer the bourbon, soy creamer, sage leaves, cloves, nutmeg, cinnamon, and pepper in a saucepan, making sure that it doesn't boil. Serve in a mug, garnished with a cinnamon stick.

CRISPY MUSHROOMS with HORSERADISH CREAM and TAPIOCA CAVIAR

The tastes and textures of this dish, made with crispy oyster mushrooms topped with smooth horseradish cream and "caviar" made with tapioca pearls, are spectacular. Serving this very elegant appetizer with a round of holiday cocktails or punch is a divine way to celebrate.

SERVES 8 TO 10

TAPIOCA CAVIAR

3 tablespoons tapioca pearls
2 tablespoons soy sauce
1 tablespoon balsamic vinegar
½ teaspoon grapeseed oil

HORSERADISH CREAM

2 tablespoons peeled and shredded fresh horseradish
½ cup silken tofu
1 tablespoon vegan cream cheese
2 tablespoons extra-virgin olive oil
2 tablespoons brown rice vinegar
1 teaspoon sea salt

2 cups unbleached all-purpose flour
1 cup yellow cornmeal
½ cup Ener-G egg replacer
1 tablespoon chopped fresh flat-leaf parsley
1 teaspoon sea salt
2 pounds oyster mushrooms, stemmed
Chopped fresh chives, to garnish

To make the tapioca caviar, bring 4 cups of water to a boil in a saucepan. Add the tapioca pearls and 1 tablespoon of the soy sauce. Decrease the heat and simmer until the pearls become translucent, about 20 minutes. Drain, rinse in cold water, and transfer to a small bowl. Add the vinegar and the remaining 1 tablespoon of soy sauce. Let the pearls soak for 3 hours at room temperature. Before serving the caviar, toss it with the grapeseed oil.

To make the horseradish cream, combine the horseradish, tofu, cream cheese, oil, vinegar, and salt in a blender and blend until smooth, 4 to 5 minutes. Cover and refrigerate for at least 20 minutes.

Preheat the oven to 350°F. Oil a baking sheet.

To make the mushrooms, combine the flour, cornmeal, egg replacer, parsley, and salt in a large bowl and mix together. Dredge the mushrooms in the flour mixture to coat completely and transfer them to the prepared baking sheet. Lightly spray the mushrooms with canola oil cooking spray.

Bake for 15 minutes, turn the mushrooms over, and continue to bake for another 15 minutes, until lightly browned. Remove from the oven and set aside to cool.

To serve, arrange the mushrooms on a large platter, drizzle with horseradish cream, and garnish with the tapioca caviar and chives.

ROASTED CAULIFLOWER and FENNEL SOUP with TRUFFLE OIL

This winter holiday soup is warm and creamy, although there is no actual cream in the recipe. A drizzle of fragrant truffle oil adds just the right finishing touch to this earthy yet decadent soup.

SERVES 8 TO 10

2 heads cauliflower (about 4 pounds), trimmed and cut into florets

3 fennel bulbs, trimmed and coarsely chopped

5 tablespoons extra-virgin olive oil

1 large white onion, thinly sliced

1 teaspoon chopped fresh flat-leaf parsley

1 teaspoon chopped fresh oregano

1 teaspoon chopped fresh thyme

6 cups vegetable stock

1 tablespoon sea salt

1/2 teaspoon white pepper

Truffle oil, to garnish

Preheat the oven to 350°F. Oil a rimmed baking sheet.

Put the cauliflower and fennel in a large bowl and toss with 2 tablespoons of the olive oil. Transfer to the prepared baking sheet and roast for about 30 minutes, until tender.

Heat the remaining 3 tablespoons of the olive oil in a large soup pot over medium-high heat. Add the onion and cook until softened, about 5 minutes. Add the parsley, oregano, and thyme and cook for 2 minutes. Add the roasted cauliflower and fennel, stock, salt, and white pepper and cook, covered, over medium heat for 20 minutes. Remove from the heat and let cool.

Transfer the soup to a blender and blend until smooth, about 5 minutes. Or transfer the mixture to a large bowl and blend with an immersion blender.

To serve, warm the soup and ladle it into bowls, drizzling each serving with truffle oil.

BRASED CRANBERRY-ORANGE TOFU

Warm roasted tofu, ruby red cranberries, and oranges pop with the delicious flavors of the season in this beautiful dish. We make this holiday favorite for both Thanksgiving and Christmas and have shared the recipe with many friends over the years.

SERVES 8 TO 10

2 tablespoons extra-virgin olive oil
2 shallots, thinly sliced
1 cup water
1 cup fresh or frozen cranberries
2 oranges, juiced
2 tablespoons agave nectar, plus more if needed
1 cup white wine
1 teaspoon sea salt
½ teaspoon freshly ground black pepper
½ teaspoon arrowroot powder dissolved in
   2 tablespoons water
Finely grated zest of two oranges
2 (14-ounce) blocks extra-firm tofu
1 sprig fresh rosemary

Heat the oil in a small sauté pan over medium heat. Add the shallots and cook until softened, about 5 minutes. Transfer the shallots to a saucepan; add the water, cranberries, orange juice, agave, wine, salt, and pepper and bring to a boil. Decrease the heat, add the arrowroot, and simmer until the cranberries burst and the sauce has slightly thickened, about 7 minutes. If the sauce seems too tart, add a bit more agave. Remove from the heat, stir in the zest, and let cool.

Preheat the oven to 350°F. Oil a large baking dish.

Cut the tofu into ¾-inch-thick slices and put them in the prepared baking dish. Pour the cranberry-orange mixture over the tofu. Turn to coat each side. Top with the rosemary and bake for about 25 minutes, until the sauce starts to caramelize. Serve immediately.

BROCCOLI RABE with SHALLOTS and HAZELNUTS

Broccoli rabe is a fantastic green that has a naturally bitter flavor. In our version, flavorful ingredients, such as garlic, shallots, and toasted hazelnuts, stand up to and enhance its delicious, pungent bite.

SERVES 8 TO 10

1 cup chopped hazelnuts
3 tablespoons extra-virgin olive oil
1 cup sliced shallots
5 cloves garlic, sliced
2 pounds broccoli rabe, stems and tough outer
  leaves trimmed
½ cup vegetable stock or water
Sea salt and freshly ground black pepper

To toast the hazelnuts, preheat the oven to 300°F. Put the nuts on a baking sheet and roast for about 10 minutes, until lightly browned. Set aside.

Heat the oil in a large sauté pan over medium-high heat, add the shallots and garlic, and cook until softened, about 5 minutes. Add the broccoli rabe and stock and cook, covered, until broccoli rabe is tender, 5 to 10 minutes. Add salt and pepper to taste and toss.

Transfer the vegetables to a plate, top with toasted hazelnuts, and serve.

POTATO GRATIN

The golden layers of earthy potatoes and vegan mozzarella cheese in this creamy gratin are a treat, and we serve it as a hearty side dish with a number of entrées all winter long. You can also add thin slices of fennel or celery root to this dish, or make it with sweet potatoes, for delicious variations.

SERVES 8 TO 10

2 pounds russet potatoes, peeled and thinly sliced
2 cups plain unsweetened soy milk
1 tablespoon chopped fresh flat-leaf parsley
1 tablespoon chopped fresh chives
1 tablespoon extra-virgin olive oil
½ teaspoon sea salt
¼ teaspoon freshly ground black pepper
½ cup dried bread crumbs
2 cups shredded vegan mozzarella cheese

Preheat the oven to 350°F. Oil a large baking dish or gratin dish.

Combine the potatoes, soy milk, parsley, chives, olive oil, salt, and pepper in a large bowl and gently toss together. Remove the potatoes with a slotted spoon and reserve the liquid.

Spread ¼ cup of the bread crumbs in the baking dish. Layer the potatoes, sprinkling each layer with cheese. Pour enough of the reserved liquid over them to come up to the top of the layers. Sprinkle with the remaining ¼ cup of the bread crumbs and cover the dish with aluminum foil.

Bake for 45 minutes, remove the foil, and bake for about 15 minutes more, until the gratin is crisp and golden on top. Serve hot.

SPICED BREAD PUDDING

We love to make warm and homey bread pudding during the winter holidays, and this recipe can be served on its own or dressed up with a drizzle of berry sauce, homemade preserves, or another sauce of your choice. We bake the pudding in loaf pans, which makes it very easy to serve and to bring to others for holiday potlucks and as delicious food gifts. Note that the raisins will need to soak overnight.

SERVES 8 TO 10

1 cup raisins
½ cup fresh orange juice
8 cups day-old sourdough bread, cubed
2 tablespoons Earth Balance Natural Buttery Spread, melted
4 cups plain unsweetened soy milk
2 cups unrefined sugar
1 teaspoon ground cinnamon
½ teaspoon freshly grated nutmeg
Raspberry Coulis (page 45) or Homemade Preserves
   (page 65), to serve (optional)

The day before serving, combine the raisins and orange juice in a small bowl, cover with water, and soak overnight in the refrigerator.

Preheat the oven to 350°F. Oil 2 (4 by 8-inch) loaf pans and set aside.

Combine the raisins and their soaking liquid, bread, buttery spread, soy milk, sugar, cinnamon, and nutmeg in a large bowl. Using your hands, mix together thoroughly, making sure the bread absorbs the liquid.

Divide the mixture between the prepared loaf pans and cover with aluminum foil. Bake for 20 minutes, remove the foil, and bake for an additional 15 minutes. Let cool for 30 minutes.

To serve, spoon the pudding onto dessert plates or into bowls and drizzle with the coulis.

CHEESE PLATE

Chef Angel is an artisan cheese maker, and his cheeses look and taste extraordinary. Making vegan cheese from scratch can seem like a daunting project, but it really isn't. You simply need to give nuts, such as cashews or macadamias, time to soak and soften before blending them. You can create a fabulous holiday cheese plate by adding fresh and dried figs, grapes, pears, and apples, an assortment of nuts, and your favorite crackers and bread to these splendid cheeses.

SERVES 8 TO 10

CASHEW CHEESE
2 cups raw cashews
2 tablespoons fresh lemon juice
1 tablespoon nutritional yeast
1 tablespoon extra-virgin olive oil
1 teaspoon sea salt
1 tablespoon chopped fresh flat-leaf parsley
1 tablespoon chopped fresh chives

MACADAMIA CHEESE
2 cups raw macadamia nuts
2 tablespoons fresh lemon juice
2 teaspoons extra-virgin olive oil
1 teaspoon sea salt
2 tablespoons pink and green peppercorns

Assorted crackers and fruit, to serve

To make the cashew cheese, the day before serving, put the cashews in a bowl and add enough cold water to cover them. Cover and let soak overnight in the refrigerator.

Drain and rinse the cashews and transfer to a food processor. Add the lemon juice, nutritional yeast, oil, and salt and blend until smooth, 10 to 12 minutes. If you find that there is not enough liquid in the food processor to blend the nuts, add a bit of water.

Transfer the cashew paste to a bowl and refrigerate for 1 hour to firm. Remove and pack the paste into a 4-inch ring mold. Remove the mold and press into the outer edges a mixture of the parsley and chives.

To make the macadamia cheese, the day before serving, put the macadamia nuts in a bowl and add enough cold water to cover them. Cover and let soak overnight in the refrigerator.

Drain and rinse the nuts and transfer to a food processor. Add the lemon juice, oil, and salt and blend until smooth, 10 to 12 minutes.

Transfer the macadamia paste to a bowl and refrigerate for 1 hour to firm. Remove and pack the paste into a 4-inch ring mold. Remove the mold and press into the

rnish

SPRITZ COOKIES

Classic spritz cookies, made with a cookie press, are the very essence of Christmas, and they are a welcome and tasty addition to your holiday cookie tray. Serve them plain or dress them up with colored sugars, sprinkles, or frosting. You can also decorate them with beautiful red dried cranberries.

MAKES ABOUT 40 COOKIES

1 cup Earth Balance Natural Buttery Spread
¾ cup unrefined sugar
2 tablespoons Ener-G egg replacer, beaten with ¼ cup water
2 cups unbleached all-purpose flour
½ teaspoon baking powder
Pinch of sea salt
1 teaspoon almond extract
Colored sugar, sprinkles, chips, or dried cranberries, for decoration

Preheat the oven to 400°F. Oil two baking sheets.

With a mixer, cream the buttery spread in a large bowl and slowly add in the sugar. Stir in the egg replacer mixture.

Sift together the flour, baking powder, and salt and gradually beat into the butter mixture until well incorporated. Stir in the almond extract.

Fit a cookie press with the desired disk, fill with the dough, and press the cookies onto the prepared baking sheets about 3 inches apart. Decorate with the desired toppings.

Bake for 10 to 12 minutes, until the edges are golden brown. Let cool on the baking sheets for 2 minutes. Then remove and let cool on a plate or cooling rack completely before serving.

GINGERBREAD MOLASSES COOKIES

Gingerbread cookies cut into a variety of shapes are a time-honored holiday tradition, and we love to bake batches of them for the whole family. The aroma of these cookies baking in the oven will fill your kitchen with warmth and happiness.

MAKES ABOUT 30 COOKIES

1 cup blackstrap molasses
1 cup packed brown sugar
1 cup Earth Balance Natural Buttery Spread
3 tablespoons Ener-G egg replacer,
   dissolved in ¼ cup water
5 cups unbleached all-purpose flour
1½ teaspoons baking soda
1 teaspoon ground ginger
1 teaspoon ground cloves
1 teaspoon ground cinnamon
Confectioners' sugar, for dusting (optional)

Combine the molasses and brown sugar in a saucepan and bring to a boil over medium-high heat.

Put the buttery spread in a large bowl and pour the hot molasses mixture over the butter. Stir until the butter is melted and let cool. Stir in the egg replacer mixture.

Sift together the flour, baking soda, ginger, cloves, and cinnamon in a bowl and stir into the molasses mixture.

Using a hand mixer, blend until the dough starts to get firm and smooth. Use your hands to knead the dough and finish mixing, adding a bit of water to the dough if it seems too dry.

Wrap the dough in plastic wrap and refrigerate overnight.

Preheat the oven to 350°F. Line two baking sheets with parchment paper.

Roll out the dough on a floured surface to a thickness of ¼ inch. Cut into shapes with cookie cutters and arrange the cookies on the baking sheets about 1 inch apart.

Bake for 8 to 10 minutes, until the cookies are crisp. Let cool on the baking sheet. Dust with confectioners' sugar and serve.

SNOWBALL COOKIES

We love the way that chocolate sauce dresses up these addictive little cookies. They are a beautiful (and delicious) addition to your tray of Christmas treats.

MAKES ABOUT 50 COOKIES

1 cup Earth Balance Natural Buttery Spread
3/4 cup confectioners' sugar, plus more for dusting
2 1/4 cups unbleached all-purpose flour, sifted
3/4 cup almond meal
1 1/2 teaspoons vanilla extract

CHOCOLATE SAUCE
1 cup plain unsweetened soy milk
1/2 cup maple syrup
1 1/2 cups vegan semisweet chocolate chips

Preheat the oven to 325°F. Line two baking sheets with parchment paper.

Using a mixer, cream the buttery spread and gradually add in the confectioners' sugar. Add the flour, almond meal, and vanilla. Mix well to make a smooth dough.

Using half a tablespoon, roll the dough into balls with your hands. Arrange the dough balls on the baking sheets about 1 inch apart. Bake for 18 to 20 minutes, until the cookies are lightly browned.

Meanwhile, make the chocolate sauce. Heat the soy milk in a saucepan over medium heat until it is very warm but not boiling. Transfer to a blender. Add the maple syrup and chocolate chips and let sit for 5 minutes, then blend until smooth.

Remove the cookies from the oven and let cool on the baking sheet. Dust with confectioners' sugar, drizzle with chocolate sauce, and serve.

CHOCOLATL and PEPPERMINT

Chocolatl, with Central American and Mexican origins, was served as a hot drink made with a bit of spice and no sugar. Today, hot chocolate, as we know it, is a sweet, comforting drink that is usually made with dairy. We make ours with soy milk and peppermint tea, two flavors that pair well with the cocoa. We also recommend spiking it with Cognac or brandy for the grown-ups.

SERVES 1

5 ounces plain unsweetened soy milk
1 tablespoon natural cocoa powder
1 1/2 teaspoons loose peppermint tea leaves
2 ounces Cognac or brandy (optional)
1 candy cane, to garnish

Combine the soy milk, cocoa powder, and tea leaves in a small saucepan over low heat and heat, stirring occasionally, until the mixture just begins to bubble. Strain into a mug and add the Cognac. Garnish with a candy cane and serve.

Variation: To make enough for 8, combine 5 cups soy milk, 1/2 cup cocoa powder, and 1/4 cup loose peppermint tea leaves in a large saucepan over low heat and heat, stirring occasionally, until the mixture just begins to bubble. Strain the mixture into a thermos to keep warm. Add 2 ounces Cognac to each of the 8 servings, garnish each with a candy cane, and serve.

NEW YEAR'S EVE

Say good-bye to the old year and ring in the new with a delicious celebration to share with friends and family. Whether you're serving an intimate romantic dinner or hosting a big New Year's Eve bash, our elegant menu is full of sumptuous dishes with something for everyone. From the first festive cocktail to the last bite of warm apple turnover with champagne ice cream, your guests will remember this party all year long. Happy New Year!

LADY DAY

What better way to ring in the New Year than with a great bubbly cocktail? Prepare a vodka infusion made with berries and vanilla a few days ahead of time, mix it with sparkling wine, and serve with a garnish of beautiful berries on the big night. When making the infusion, try to use a brand of vodka that has herbal notes, such as Fair or Death's Door. Note that the infusion makes enough vodka and berries for 18 cocktails.

SERVES 1

BERRY AND VANILLA VODKA INFUSION
2 cups fresh or frozen cranberries, thawed if frozen
2 cups fresh or frozen blueberries or huckleberries
1 whole vanilla bean
1 (750-ml) bottle vodka

1 ounce fresh lime juice
1 ounce agave nectar
White or rosé sparkling wine

Combine all berries and the vanilla pod in a clean container and pour in the vodka. Cover tightly and let it infuse for 3 days. Strain into a pitcher, reserve the berries, and discard the vanilla bean. The infused vodka and berries will keep in separate mason jars in the refrigerator for up to a week.

Combine 1½ ounces of the infused vodka, the lime juice, and agave in a mixing glass and stir together with a bar spoon. Pour into a champagne flute and top with sparkling wine. Garnish with some of the reserved berries and serve.

POM PALM

Whether you're welcoming in the New Year or simply slow-sipping a tasty drink on a cold winter's night, you will enjoy this cocktail made with rye and pomegranate juice. We prefer Koval Dark Rye, a small-batch whiskey that is distilled in Chicago. It has beautiful notes of oak.

SERVES 1

2 ounces dark rye whiskey
2 ounces pomegranate juice
½ ounce agave nectar
½ ounce fresh lime juice
Ice
1 mint leaf, to garnish

Combine the rye, pomegranate juice, agave, and lime juice in a cocktail shaker. Add ice, shake well, and strain into a martini glass. Garnish with a mint leaf and serve.

BLINI with CRÈME FRAÎCHE and HIJIKI CAVIAR

Blini and caviar are a New Year's tradition, and we love to serve these lovely little pancakes topped with vegan crème fraîche and caviar made with hijiki during cocktail hour. You can make the toppings and the blini batter ahead of time so everything will be ready when it's time to cook and assemble this dish.

SERVES 8 TO 10

CRÈME FRAÎCHE
2 cups vegan cream cheese
1 cup silken tofu
2 tablespoons fresh lemon juice
¼ cup water
½ teaspoon sea salt

HIJIKI CAVIAR
½ cup hijiki or arame sea vegetable
1 tablespoon tamari
1½ teaspoons grapeseed oil
1½ teaspoons fresh lemon juice
¼ teaspoon chopped garlic
3 tablespoons chopped fresh chives

1½ cups unbleached all-purpose flour
2 tablespoons baking powder
1 tablespoon Ener-G egg replacer,
   dissolved in 2 tablespoons water
½ teaspoon sea salt
¼ teaspoon freshly ground black pepper
2 cups plain unsweetened soy milk
¼ teaspoon vanilla extract
½ cup Earth Balance Natural Buttery Spread, melted
½ cup cooked quinoa
1 tablespoon safflower oil, plus more as needed

To make the crème fraîche, combine the cream cheese, tofu, lemon juice, water, and salt in a blender and blend until smooth. Refrigerate for 1 hour.

To make the hijiki caviar, put the hijiki in a bowl and cover with 4 cups of cold water. Let soak until all the seaweed has expanded and softened, 30 to 40 minutes.

Rinse and drain the hijiki in a colander and let it sit for a few minutes to dry. Blot the excess water with a paper towel. Transfer the hijiki to a cutting board and very finely chop.

Whisk together the tamari, oil, lemon juice, garlic, and 2 tablespoons of the chives in a medium bowl and let sit for 20 minutes to allow the flavors to meld together. Set aside. Add the hijiki and refrigerate for at least 1 hour, or overnight.

To make the blini, combine the flour, baking powder, egg replacer mixture, salt, and pepper in a large bowl and stir together. Add the soy milk, vanilla, buttery spread, and quinoa and mix together thoroughly. The batter can be made ahead and will keep, covered, in the refrigerator for up to a day. Bring to room temperature before cooking.

Heat the oil in a nonstick skillet over medium-low heat. Add 1 tablespoon of the batter to the pan. Cook on each side until golden brown, 1 to 2 minutes. Repeat with the remaining batter, adding more oil if necessary.

To serve, arrange the blini on a platter. Top them with crème fraîche and hijiki caviar and garnish with the remaining chives.

VEGETABLE BLACK-EYED PEA SOUP

According to Southern folklore, black-eyed peas bring good luck, and if they are the first food eaten in the New Year they will bring prosperity to you and your family. Whether or not the superstition holds true, eating this earthy and nourishing soup is simply a great way to end and start the year.

SERVES 8 TO 10

2 cups black-eyed peas, rinsed and soaked in water to
    cover for 4 hours
8 cups water
2 bay leaves
2 tablespoons extra-virgin olive oil
2 cloves garlic, chopped
1 cup diced leeks, white and pale green parts
1 cup peeled and diced sweet potatoes
1 cup peeled and diced celeriac or parsnips
1 cup unseasoned tomato sauce
4 dried guajillo chiles
8 cups vegetable stock
2 cups stemmed and chopped kale
¼ teaspoon smoked paprika
1 tablespoon chopped fresh cilantro
1 tablespoon sea salt

Drain the beans and set aside.

Bring the water to a boil in a large pot and add the beans and bay leaves. Decrease the heat to medium-high and cook until the beans are tender, about 1 hour. Drain the beans, discard the bay leaf, and set aside.

Heat the olive oil in a large soup pot over medium-high heat. Add the garlic, leeks, sweet potatoes, and celeriac and cook until softened, about 10 minutes.

Combine the tomato sauce and chiles in a blender and blend until smooth, 3 to 5 minutes. Transfer to the soup pot, add the stock, and simmer for 10 minutes. Add the beans, kale, paprika, cilantro, and salt. Cook for 10 minutes, stirring occasionally. Taste and adjust the seasonings, if necessary, and serve. The soup will keep in the refrigerator for up to 3 days and in the freezer for up to 1 month.

BELUGA LENTIL SALAD with
GREEN BEANS, GRAPES, and CHAMPAGNE VINAIGRETTE

It feels like caviar and champagne are on the menu when you serve this elegant salad that glistens with black beluga lentils and a drizzle of tart and tasty champagne vinaigrette.

SERVES 8 TO 10

1 cup beluga lentils, rinsed, picked over, and soaked in water
   for 2 to 4 hours
¼ teaspoon sea salt
1 pound green beans, trimmed
2 tablespoons chopped fresh flat-leaf parsley
2 tablespoons chopped fresh chives
¾ cup sliced red grapes
¾ cup sliced green grapes
½ cup pomegranate seeds

VINAIGRETTE

1 tablespoon extra-virgin olive oil
1 cup chopped shallots
1 cup grapeseed oil
½ cup champagne vinegar
½ teaspoon sea salt
½ teaspoon freshly ground black pepper

1 pound baby arugula, to serve

Drain the lentils.

Bring 4 cups of water to a boil and add the lentils and salt. Cook over medium-high heat until the lentils are tender, 15 to 20 minutes. Drain and let cool.

In a clean pot, bring 4 cups of water to a boil. Add the green beans and cook until just tender, about 5 minutes. Drain and rinse with cold water.

Combine the lentils, green beans, parsley, and chives in a large bowl and toss together. Toss the grapes and pomegranate seeds together in another bowl.

To make the vinaigrette, heat the olive oil in a sauté pan over medium heat. Add the shallots and cook until softened, about 5 minutes. Transfer to a blender, add the grapeseed oil, vinegar, salt, and pepper and blend until smooth, 3 to 5 minutes.

Add the dressing to the bean mixture and toss together.

Arrange the arugula on salad plates, top with the lentil and bean mixture and the grapes and pomegranate seeds, and serve.

HOMEMADE PAPPARDELLE with SPINACH, PORTOBELLO MUSHROOMS, and ROASTED RED PEPPER SAUCE

In Tuscan dialect, pappardelle *comes from the word* papparsi, *and it literally means to gobble up or to stuff oneself. That's very easy to do when eating these wide ribbons of homemade pasta laced with red pepper sauce, spinach, and mushrooms. It's best to make the sauce ahead of time and to prepare the spinach mixture while the pasta is cooking because the pasta, vegetables, and sauce should be tossed together very quickly just before serving.*

SERVES 8 TO 10

RED PEPPER SAUCE
6 red bell peppers
3 tablespoons extra-virgin olive oil
1 white onion, sliced
2 cloves garlic
4 cups water
½ teaspoon white pepper
1 tablespoon sea salt
1 tablespoon Earth Balance Natural Buttery Spread

PAPPARDELLE
2 cups brown rice flour
2 cups semolina flour
2 cups whole wheat pastry flour
7 ounces silken tofu
2 cups water
4 tablespoons extra-virgin olive oil
1 tablespoon plus 1½ teaspoons sea salt

3 tablespoons extra-virgin olive oil
¾ cup sliced shallots
4 cloves garlic, chopped
1 pound portobello mushrooms, stemmed and thinly sliced
1 tablespoon Earth Balance Natural Buttery Spread
1 pound baby spinach
12 chopped fresh basil leaves

Preheat the oven to 350°F.

To make the sauce, spray the peppers with canola cooking spray, arrange them on a baking sheet, and roast for 30 to 40 minutes, until they begin to soften. Remove from the oven and let cool. With a peeler or a sharp knife, peel the skins and remove the seeds. Set aside.

Heat the olive oil in a large pot over medium heat. Add the onion and garlic and cook until the onion is translucent, 5 to 8 minutes. Add the red peppers, water, white pepper, salt, and buttery spread to the pot. Cook, stirring occasionally, until the vegetables are soft, 20 to 30 minutes. Remove from the heat and let cool.

Transfer the sauce mixture to a blender and blend until smooth, 5 to 8 minutes. The sauce can be made ahead of time and will keep, covered, in the refrigerator for up to 2 days. Slowly simmer the sauce before serving.

To make the pappardelle, combine the flours, tofu, water, 2 tablespoons of the oil, and 1½ teaspoons of the salt in a stand mixer fitted with a dough hook and mix together, starting at slow speed and slowly escalating to medium, until the dough is firm, 5 to 8 minutes. Remove and form the dough into 6 balls.

Dust a flat surface with a bit of brown rice and semolina flours. Roll a ball of the dough into a 12-inch-long rectangle, about ⅛ inch thick. With a knife, cut the dough into ¼-inch strips lengthwise. Transfer the strips to a baking sheet and cover with a damp cloth. Repeat with the remaining dough. *continued*

Bring 16 cups of water to a boil in a large pot and add the remaining 2 tablespoons of olive oil and 1 tablespoon of salt. Add the pasta and cook until just tender, 3 to 4 minutes. Drain and return to the pot.

Meanwhile, to prepare the spinach and mushrooms, heat the 3 tablespoons of olive oil in a sauté pan over medium-high heat. Add the shallots, garlic, and mushrooms and cook until softened, 5 to 8 minutes. Add the buttery spread, spinach, and basil leaves and cook until the spinach is just wilted, 2 to 3 minutes.

Add the vegetables and the warm sauce to the pasta and toss together until the pasta is well coated. Serve immediately.

TRUFFLE TOFU MEDALLIONS with WILD MUSHROOM and PINOT GRIS SAUCE

What an elegant way to celebrate the New Year! This rich and tasty tofu dish is infused overnight with truffle oil and topped with a savory wild mushroom and wine sauce. Serve with brussels sprouts, fresh asparagus, or green beans.

SERVES 8 TO 10

2 (14-ounce) blocks extra-firm tofu
2 cups water
2/3 cup grapeseed oil
1 teaspoon truffle oil
2 tablespoons fresh lemon juice
1/2 teaspoon chopped fresh chives
1 1/2 teaspoons sea salt
1/2 teaspoon freshly ground black pepper
3 tablespoons extra-virgin olive oil

WILD MUSHROOM & PINOT GRIS SAUCE
2 tablespoons extra-virgin olive oil
1/2 cup sliced shallots
1/2 cup finely chopped oyster mushrooms
1/2 cup finely chopped trumpet royale mushrooms
1/2 cup finely chopped portobello mushrooms
1/4 teaspoon fresh oregano
1/2 teaspoon sea salt
1/4 teaspoon freshly ground black pepper
1 tablespoon unbleached all-purpose flour
1/2 cup Pinot Gris

The day before you plan to serve, slice each block of tofu into 10 squares. Whisk together the water, grapeseed oil, truffle oil, lemon juice, chives, salt, and pepper in a bowl. Add the tofu, stir to coat, cover, and marinate in the refrigerator overnight.

Remove the tofu from the marinade with a slotted spoon and reserve the marinade.

Heat the olive oil in a large sauté pan over medium-high heat. Add the tofu and cook until lightly browned, 3 to 4 minutes per side. Set aside.

To make the sauce, heat the olive oil in a large sauté pan over medium-high heat. Add the shallots and all of the mushrooms. Cook until the shallots start to brown, 5 to 6 minutes. Add the oregano, salt, pepper, and flour. Cook, stirring constantly, so the shallots and mushrooms are coated, for 3 minutes. Add the wine and cook, stirring, until the wine begins to simmer and reduce, about 3 minutes. Add 3 tablespoons of the reserved tofu marinade and cook until the sauce is slightly thickened, about 5 minutes. Taste and adjust the seasonings, if necessary.

To serve, put 2 pieces of tofu on each plate and top with sauce.

WARM APPLE TURNOVERS and CHAMPAGNE ICE CREAM

It's a nice touch to end a lavish dinner party with something simple for dessert. And what could be simpler than little warm turnovers filled with apples and cinnamon? Top them with scoops of elegant champagne ice cream for a comforting conclusion to a wonderful year.

SERVES 8 TO 10

CHAMPAGNE ICE CREAM
1 cup plain unsweetened soy milk
1 cup soy creamer
½ cup safflower oil
1 cup coconut milk
1 cup unrefined sugar
1 cup champagne

APPLE FILLING
8 apples, peeled, cored, and thinly sliced
2 teaspoons Earth Balance Natural Buttery Spread
¼ cup unrefined sugar, plus more for sprinkling
½ teaspoon ground cinnamon
1 teaspoon arrowroot powder mixed with
  2 tablespoons water

DOUGH
6 cups unbleached all-purpose flour
2 cups palm oil, melted
1 cup vegan cream cheese
2 teaspoons ground cinnamon
¼ cup unrefined sugar
2 cups water
2 tablespoons Earth Balance Natural Buttery Spread,
  melted, for brushing

Whisk together the soy milk, soy creamer, oil, coconut milk, and sugar in a bowl. Transfer to a large saucepan and bring to a boil over medium-high heat. Remove from the heat, whisk again, and slowly add the champagne while whisking. Strain the mixture into a bowl through a fine sieve.

Transfer the mixture to an ice cream maker and freeze according to the manufacturer's instructions. Remove and store in a bowl in the freezer for at least an hour and up to a week.

To make the filling, combine the apples, buttery spread, sugar, and cinnamon in a saucepan over medium heat and cook, stirring constantly, until the apples are tender, about 5 minutes. Stir in the arrowroot mixture and set aside.

To make the dough, combine the flour, oil, cream cheese, cinnamon, sugar, and water in a large bowl. Mix together until combined and form into 2 balls. Roll out each ball of the dough on a work surface lightly dusted with flour into an 8- by 12-inch rectangle. Transfer both rectangles of dough to a baking sheet covered with lightly dusted parchment paper, then cover the dough with another sheet. Refrigerate for 20 minutes.

Preheat the oven to 350°F. Oil a baking sheet.

Remove the dough from the refrigerator and lay out on a floured surface. Cut each rectangle into 6 (4-inch) squares.

Spoon about ¼ cup of the apple filling onto half of each square and fold the dough over to make a triangle. Press the edges with a fork to seal. Transfer the turnovers to the prepared baking sheet, brush them with the buttery spread, and sprinkle with sugar. Bake for about 20 minutes, until golden brown. Serve 1 or 2 warm turnovers on a dish with a scoop of ice cream.

Resource Guide

BEER AND SPIRITS

Butte Creek Brewing
www.buttecreek.com
California brewer of organic beers

Fair Spirits
www.fairspirits.com
*Quinoa-based vodka and other
sustainable spirits*

Greenbar Craft Distillery
www.greenbar.biz
*Organic and ecofriendly liquors, such as
Crusoe Rum, TruVodka, and Citry
Orange Liqueur*

Greenhook Gin
www.greenhookgin.com
*Artisan, sustainable gin made in
Brooklyn, New York*

Ilegal Mezcal
www.ilegalmezcal.com
Sustainable, hand-crafted mezcal

Koval Distillery
www.koval-distillery.com
*Chicago distiller of sustainable whiskeys,
bourbons, and ryes*

Puro Verde Spirits
www.puroverdespirits.com
Organic tequilas

Sam Smith Brewery
www.samuelsmithbrewery.co.uk
British brewer of organic beers and ciders

VeeV
www.veevlife.com
Açai-based spirits

FLAVOR AND SWEETENERS

Bionaturae
www.bionaturae.com
Organic fruit nectars

da Rosario
www.darosario.com
Organic truffle oil

Enjoy Life
www.enjoylifefood.com
Dairy-, soy-, and nut-free chocolate chips

Flavorganics
www.flavorganics.com
Organic syrups and flavor extracts

Los Chileros de Nuevo Mexico
www.loschileros.com
*Organic, all-natural dried chiles and
pure chile powders*

Pete's Sweets, New York Maple
www.nysmaple.com
Maple syrup from New York

Rapunzel Pure Organics
www.rapunzel.com
*Organic yeasts, chocolate, and
sugar products*

Suzanne's Sweeteners
www.suzannes-specialties.com
*Organic agave nectar, brown rice syrup,
blackstrap molasses, and other sweeteners*

South River Miso
www.southrivermiso.com
Organic miso products

Spectrum Organics
www.spectrumorganics.com
*All-natural, organic artisan oils
and spreads*

Sunspire Natural Chocolates
www.sunspire.com
*All-natural, organic, fair-trade,
dairy-free chocolate*

Wholesome Sweeteners
www.wholesomesweeteners.com
*Organic all-natural sweeteners and
unrefined sugars*

GRAINS

Lundberg Family Farms
www.lundberg.com
Rice-based products

Quinoa Corporation
www.quinoa.net
*Ancient harvest quinoa products:
organic, non-GMO, and gluten-free
quinoa, quinoa flour, and quinoa-corn
pastas*

truRoots
www.truroots.com
*Organic sprouted whole grains
and beans*

HERBS & SPICES

DiviniTea
www.divinitea.com
Organic loose-leaf tea

Frontier Natural Products
www.frontiercoop.com
Bulk organic herbs, spices, and teas

MISCELLANEOUS

Eden Foods, Inc.
www.edenfoods.com
Specialty organic products

Edward & Sons
www.edwardandsons.com
Organic and vegan specialties, coconut milk, and coconut cream

Ener-G Foods Inc.
www.ener-g.com
Gluten-free specialty foods and egg replacer

Goldmine Natural Food Company
www.goldminenaturalfood.com
Organic and heirloom foods

Navitas Naturals
www.navitasnaturals.com
Organic cashews, cacao, wakame, nori, fruits, and berries

Twin Marquis
www.twinmarquis.com
Asian specialty items, including vegan wonton wrappers

Whole Foods
www.wholefoods.com
Largest retailer of natural and organic foods

PRODUCE

Earthbound Farms
www.ebfarm.com
Non-GMO and organic salads, fruits, and vegetables

Four Seasons Produce, Inc.
www.fsproduce.com
Organic produce

Fungus Among Us
www.fungusamongus.com
Organic dried mushrooms

Melissa's
www.melissas.com
Organic produce and chiles

Maine Coast Sea Vegetables
www.seaveg.com
Sea vegetables

Satur Farms
www.saturfarms.com
Specialty salad greens, leafy vegetables, heirloom tomatoes, root vegetables, and herbs, grown in Long Island and available online

PROTEINS

Field Roast Grain Meat Co.
www.fieldroast.com
Artisan and vegan grain-based meats and sausages

Follow Your Heart
www.followyourheart.com
Veganaise and vegan cheeses

Fresh Tofu Inc.
www.freshtofu.com
Certified organic tofu, tempeh, and seitan

Turtle Island Foods
www.tofurkey.com
Makers of Tofurkey vegan sausages and meat substitutes

TOOLS

Breville
www.brevilleusa.com
Blenders, immersion blenders, and juicers

Vitamix
www.vitamix.com
Vitamix blender

VEGAN BUTTER, CREAMS, AND CHEESES

Daiya Foods, Inc.
www.daiyafoods.com
Allergen-free tapioca-based cheese

Earth Balance
www.earthbalancenatural.com
Dairy-free butters, spreads, and milks

Westsoy
www.westsoymilk.com
Organic soy milk

Acknowledgments

OUR ATTITUDE IS CONSTANT GRATITUDE

We know that the key to hosting a great party is to serve great food, invite wonderful guests, and have a great team of people to work with. We are so fortunate to have all of that each and every day.

At our Candle restaurants we have the honor and privilege to put on a party every night, and holidays are even more special. We consider our guests to be part of our extended family, and we truly enjoy hosting them and celebrating together. They were our inspiration for creating this vegan holiday cookbook so they can cook and share vegan food in their own homes for all occasions. We thank them—four generations, and counting—for dining with us and supporting us year after year.

Everything that we are and that we do originates from our restaurants, and this book would not be made possible without the tireless efforts and many talents of the hundred-plus people on our Candle team that make our restaurants run smoothly every day. The dedication, leadership, and warm hospitality of general managers Benay Vynerib, Gabriela Martinez Benecke, and Angela Mignone along with the creativity and cooking skills of our lead chefs, Eugenio Miranda and Delfino Alvarez, create a unity of vision and spirit that makes us whole and this book possible.

We are now in our thirtieth year of serving incredible vegan organic food and we thank our "village" of suppliers, including Lisa and Mark Dunau of Mountain Dell Farm, Guy Jones of Blooming Hill Farm, Paulette Satur and Eberhard Muller of Satur Farms, and Josh Steinhauer of Four Seasons. We are also grateful to Kathy Lavigne and Tor Newman of Ace Natural, who deliver their top-of-the-line organic goods daily to our chefs and bartenders, to Linda Smith of Divinitea for her fine tea blends and her expertise, and to Mimi Clark, Alison Cox, and Joel Dee of Edward & Sons for their ongoing encouragement, support, and friendship. We also thank Judith Wendell of Sacred Currents for blessing us along the way and for honoring our sacred food and space.

Special thanks go to our eco-mixologists, led by Gabriela Martinez Benecke and Dianne de la Veaux, for bringing that extra kick and fun to the party with creations crafted with love and compassion. Their unique blends of sustainable spirits and fresh ingredients truly bring the organic farm to the bar. And thanks to our teams of bartenders at Candle 79 and Candle Cafe West, who get the party started and keep it going with their inspirational cocktails. Many thanks also to Elizabeth Corradino for her expert legal advice and guidance and to Eric Adjei and Ishmael Adam for paying the bills on time and keeping us on point.

We are grateful to the many talented people who worked on this book. Thanks to Kim DeJesus who took the raw ideas from our chefs and shaped them into recipes; to our recipe testers who worked with such care and precision to make every dish delicious and clear for the home cook: Lisa Dawn Angerame, Kim Baron, Anja Riebensahm, Annette Doskow, Lynn Doskow, Heather DeSantis, Lottie Bildirici, Rosella Galli, Sarah Gianella, Stephanie Fields and her daughter Jessie, and Andrea Sperling; and to the Candle 79 bartenders for testing the cocktails. And thanks to Wendy and Ben for their ongoing love and support and for always being there throughout the years. Your input and nutritional knowledge and research is always appreciated.

Many thanks to photographer Jim Franco and his talented team who created images that capture the beauty and fun of our food, to food stylist Chris Barsch who helped make every dish look wonderful, to our bartenders Andrew McNeal and Stephen King for making the cocktails look fantastic, and to prop stylist Kate Parisian whose eye and beautiful sense of style were spot on. You all made it work!

And many thanks to Barbara Scott-Goodman whose sensibility, care, and keen eye is invaluable to our process and who once again helped channel our work to a whole new level, and to Margot Schupf who started us on this book journey that we are now addicted to. Thanks for opening the door for us to share our recipes and for always being available when we have questions or need a hand. Many thanks to Mark Doskow and his entire growing family who tasted and tested for us and who kept this whole project on track from start to finish.

We thank the incredible team at Ten Speed Press: Aaron Wehner, Lisa Westmoreland, Toni Tajima, Michele Crim, and Kara Van de Water for their sharp editorial and design work and marketing expertise, and for their insight, patience, and support.

Much love and many thanks go to our immediate and extended families, Rosie, Jerry, and Juni Pineda, the Ramos family, Laura, Woody, Zoe, Deni, Makani, Alicia, Christopher, Bear, Grant, Laura, Scarlett Rose, Maren, Kris, Gene, Jimmy, Micki, Franki, and Liz Rosen. And to Dylan, Leia, Wyatt, Silas, and all the future generations for giving us an infinite number of reasons to do what we do.

Cheers to Candle founder, Bart Potenza, the Godfather who makes life bright and all things possible. Constant gratitude for your unwavering support and love.

About the Authors

JOY PIERSON is a nutritionist and co-owner of the Candle Cafe, Candle Cafe West, and Candle 79. Her passion for counseling and healing through great food led her to join Bart Potenza at the Healthy Candle in 1988, where they began creating foods and menus tailored to the nutritional needs of clients from Joy's private practice and the Healthy Candle's ever-growing customer base. Their partnership flourished and they have since created three restaurants, a growing catering and wholesale business, and two books, *The Candle Cafe Cookbook* and *Candle 79 Cookbook.* Joy graduated from Tufts University magna cum laude, has been a nutritional counselor since 1985, and is certified by the Pritikin Longevity Center and Hippocrates Health Institute. In addition to time spent at the restaurants, Joy avidly promotes their mission beyond the restaurants' walls. She has written and lectured extensively about food and nutrition, sharing her expertise with an ever-widening audience as more people become mindful of the positive effects of healthful eating. She regularly leads workshops and teaches courses on diet and nutrition. Joy has appeared on the *Today* show, *Good Day New York, CBS News This Morning,* and the Food Network's *TV Food Diners,* and she has been a radio guest on *The Joan Hamburg Show, The Howard Stern Show, The Marilu Henner Show,* and NPR. Joy is board cochair of the New York Coalition for Healthy School Lunches and on the advisory board for Wellness in the Schools. Her quest is to continue changing people's awareness of health and well-being and its effect on the planet and future generations by bringing farm-fresh vegan food to as many people and as many tables as possible! Joy lives in New York City.

Executive Chef **ANGEL RAMOS** cultivated his talents for eight years at Candle Cafe. He then brought the innovative creations that he perfected at the Cafe with him to Candle 79 and Candle Cafe West, and he has continued to take vegan cooking to new creative heights with a flair for combining the right mix of flavors and textures with multicultural influences. Chef Ramos has been acknowledged by the *New York Times* for his mastery of vegan organic cuisine, and he has consulted with other chefs on the menus for galas at the Plaza, Cipriani on Wall Street, and the Beverly Hills Hotel. In 2010, Angel was named the *VegNews* Chef of the Year and received an honorable mention from "People's Platelist" on ABC's *Nightline,* in which viewers selected their favorite chefs. He has twice been honored to have his food featured at events at the James Beard House. Chef Ramos has helped develop Candle Cafe Frozen Entrées, which are available nationwide at Whole Foods Market, and is a coauthor of the *Candle 79 Cookbook.* He lives in Queens, New York.

Executive Chef **JORGE PINEDA** was an instrumental part of opening Candle 79 in 2003 and Candle Cafe West in 2012 with pastries that have revolutionized vegan baking. In addition to creating the desserts and the famous house-made ice creams at Candle 79, Chef Pineda is still delighting his loyal Candle Cafe customers with his cookies, cakes, pies, and other delicious, "hard to believe they're vegan" comfort foods. Chef Pineda was a major contributor to the *Candle Cafe Cookbook* and coauthor of the *Candle 79 Cookbook*. He has also helped develop the Candle Cafe line of vegan desserts and frozen entrées for Whole Foods Market. His work has been featured in the *Los Angeles Times* as the "Best Vegan Desserts in America." Chef Pineda has been a powerful force in working with the NYC Department of Education and the Coalition for Healthy School Food in ensuring that all our children have tasty plant-based options. He teaches workshops with kids and assists in the development of recipes for schools. He also teaches at Macy's Cellar and the DeGustibus School. He lives in Fort Lee, New Jersey.

Angel Ramos, Joy Pierson, and Jorge Pineda

Index